Working Ethics

Marvin T. Brown

WORKING ETHICS

Strategies for
Decision Making and
Organizational
Responsibility

Regent Press
2000

Library of Congress Cataloging-in-Publication Data

ISBN 1-889059-55-2

Manufactured in the United States of America
Regent Press
6020-A Adeline
Oakland, CA 94608
regent@sirius.com
www.sirius.com/~regent

Contents

Preface

Ethics is a human activity. As with most activities, we can improve our performance with practice. Just as managers and teachers need to practice before they become competent, we need to practice ethics too. Like managing and teaching, studying and using ethics does not primarily produce a product but engages one in a process — a decision-making process of discovering what should be done.

Sometimes this activity results in the writing of documents, guides, or even pronouncements; but these should not become a substitute for the activity itself. The best ethical guides do not tell people what they should do; rather, they show people how to discover the best course of action for themselves. *Working Ethics* is designed to be such a guide.

Recent developments in business and organizational ethics have disguised the role of ethics in decision making. Instead of becoming involved in the process of ethical reflection, employees and managers have used ethics to control and monitor behavior. One major California corporation, for example, now requires its employees to sign an "ethics code," in which they promise that they will notify management whenever they observe a worker violating any of the code's provisions. Such attempts to make ethics work not only give ethics a bad name but also prevent members of organizations from using ethics appropriately. Ethics belongs in the decision-making processes of an organization. It can actually increase the resources for making decisions there and ensure that people make the best decisions possible.

Although this may sound odd, the purpose of ethics is not to make people ethical; it is to help people make better decisions. Decisions about what groups or organizations should do — policy decisions — can benefit from ethical reflection. When you think of the consequences that organizational decisions have for us, it becomes clear that decision makers need all the help they can get. *Working Ethics* provides some help by (1) laying out the process of ethical reflection so people can use it with their own issues, (2) connecting ethical notions such as rights and justice to the management of systems of power so people can manage these systems appropriately, (3) showing how to analyze and evaluate the different components of the decision-making process so people will have as many good resources available as possible, and (4) offering methods of developing an organizational climate in which ethical reflection can be practiced and improved.

Who Should Read This Book

This book is written primarily for people who will benefit from an ethical analysis of organizational decision making. Managers, under pressure from various sources, will discover new resources for negotiating with different groups. People involved in human resources, personnel training, communication, and labor relations will find comprehensive strategies to create the conditions necessary for responsible employee participation in organizational life. For them, the book offers a methodology for empowering employees. People concerned with designing human systems, such as organizational development consultants and senior managers, can learn how to use the concepts of social justice and individual rights as guidelines for the distribution of organizational power. All of these groups will discover how to integrate ethical practices into the ongoing processes of their organizations. I encourage these readers to use the material in each chapter to interpret their own issues and situations. The book also addresses faculty and students of business, private or public management, and organizational studies. Although they may not have organizational experiences, they still can become competent in practicing ethical analysis and discerning the conditions required for organizational justice. Finally, the growing number of people in different kinds of organizations who are interested in ethics will understand the differences between an ethics of rules, which attempts to control behavior, and an ethics of decision making, which empowers people and organizations.

Overview of the Contents

Chapter One establishes the framework for the book by showing what people need to consider in developing working ethics: the place of ethics in the decision-making process, the power dynamics of the organizational system and how justice and individual rights can serve as guidelines for maintaining the system, and the role of basic assumptions in the development of responsible organizations.

Chapter Two develops an ethical perspective as a way of interpreting ourselves, others, and organizations. The perspective allows us to see people as moral agents who can be responsible and organizations as moral communities and moral agents. The chapter reviews some current views of corporate moral agency through an analysis of who was responsible for the Valdez oil spill.

Chapter Three presents an argumentative model for ethical reflection. It examines the decision-making process and shows the necessity of value judgments and assumptions in making policy decisions. It then shows how to include opposing views so that they function as resources for making better decisions. The chapter concludes by illustrating how to use the argumentative model in a debate about whether corporate constituencies should have representation on corporate boards.

Chapter Four picks up the issue of opposing views and shows how to locate them in the context of basic agreements. It offers strategies for using the strengths of opposing views to improve the process of finding the best decision. This chapter, as well as the book as a whole, shows that differences should be taken not as threats or competitive factors in finding answers but as opportunities to increase one's knowledge and broaden one's understanding. The chapter closes by showing, through a discussion on worker participation, how to deal with disagreements.

Chapter Five explores ethical approaches for analyzing policy issues and decisions. It discusses a case that raises the question of what to do after making a mistake and shows how the ethical approaches—an ethics of purpose, principle, or consequence—would have us interpret the case. The chapter shows how these three approaches actually complement each other and how, taken together, they can increase the likelihood of making the right decision.

Chapter Six addresses one aspect of decision making rarely considered in ethics books: the analysis of factual statements. It presents topics such as the relationships between parts and whole, cause and effect, generalizations and specifics, abstract and concrete, and comparison and contrast and shows how knowledge of these relationships can make the use of the ethical approaches presented in Chapter Five much more effective.

Chapter Seven concerns the ethics of systems. It analyzes the dynamics of systems—system-environment interaction, negative entropy, and steady state—and shows the relevance of these concepts for the issue of corporate constituency relationships and for understanding corporate power. Then, using as examples temporary workers and other issues, it shows that organizations have a responsibility to maintain their power as an integrative force that empowers the whole organization. Power by itself, however, does not have any guidance system, so to determine how power should be used or distributed, it is necessary to turn to the concepts of rights and justice.

Chapter Eight explains why rights and justice belong together as criteria to guide system maintenance and power relations. It discusses the question of how to justify inequality in large organizational systems and shows what contemporary views of justice say about inequality. The chapter then turns to the question of different kinds of rights that corporate employees have and how they compare with corporate rights.

Chapter Nine provides a way to analyze basic assumptions, especially assumptions concerning how things work out or get done. One such assumption might be "what goes around comes around." It also gives methods for handling decision-making situations in which people share similar values but have different assumptions and situations in which people share assumptions but have different values. This chapter gives decision makers the means to gain access to the basic assumptions that play a role in the decision-making process.

Chapter Ten focuses on one set of assumptions that is particularly important for decision making and the process of ethical reflection: our assumptions about communication in organizations. The method of analysis presented here will allow people to understand why they find it easier to talk about values or raise critical questions in some groups than in others. With this understanding, people can begin to see what changes are necessary to create conditions for ethical reflection.

Chapter Eleven provides some guidelines for getting ethics to work. First it describes some of the conditions necessary for practicing ethical reflection in organizations, and then it provides some plans and exercises for training others in the process of ethical reflection. With Chapter Eleven, the book completes its task of providing material to train people in organizations to practice ethical reflection.

Conclusion

I have taught mainly adult students, whose organizational issues provided the context for much of this book. I have also worked as a consultant, usually developing training sessions intended to help employees gain access to their own resources for reflection and decision making. From my experience, I know that ethical reflection can empower people and increase their responsiveness to important organizational and social issues. When people become aware of their choices and have the resources to choose and to carry out the best ones, they contribute to the development of a more humane society. Engaging in ethical reflection is a learning process and can create a learning and changing organization.

Acknowledgments

Working Ethics has developed from the many classes and seminars in which I have worked with others on understanding how to get ethics to work. I am grateful for these opportunities and for the many students who have contributed to the development of the ideas and analytical tools in the book. Like most who continue to teach, I am indebted to teachers who have shown me the craft. Edward Hobbs, Paul Lehmann, and L. E. Mattingly have been especially significant. I am also grateful to my friends Stanley Brown, Rae Levine, Michael Maeder, John Moyer, Lee Townsend, and Gene Ulansky for reviewing earlier versions of this book. I am especially indebted to my father-in-law, Eberhard Müller, who years ago taught me to take organizational life seriously. I also want to express my gratitude to my parents, Thomas and Mildred Brown. Finally, I am deeply grateful to Erdmut, my wife and dear friend, who has given steady support and valuable criticisms. I dedicate this book to her and to Mark and Kirsten.

Berkeley, California   Marvin T. Brown
August 1990

The Author

Marvin T. Brown has almost twenty years experience as a teacher and consultant in organizational ethics and communication. He currently teaches at the University of San Francisco in their Philosophy Department and College of Professional Studies; at the California School of Professional Psychology in their Ph.D. organizational psychology program; and at John F. Kennedy University's school of management.

From 1994 to 1997, he served as a designer and facilitator of the Diversity and Ethics Program at Levi-Strauss and Company – a program that incorporated the decision-making process outlined in this book. During this time, he also developed more worksheets and exercises to teach and use the process. These worksheets are now incorporated in *The Ethical Process: An Approach to Controversial Issues.* This workbook – now in its second edition–is available from Prentice Hall.

Marvin T. Brown has conducted workshops and facilitated discussions on ethical decision making in the United States, Germany, Poland, Venezuela and Argentina.

He holds a BA in Religion and Philosophy, a MDiv in Practical Theology, and a Ph.D. in Theology and Rhetoric. He lives in Berkeley, California.

Working Ethics

To learn more about the process of decision making outlined here as well as about resources for using this process in your workplace, visit our website:

Workingethics.com

Chapter One

Confronting Ethical Concerns of Organizations

As we approach the next century, we are challenged by a growing concern about the morality of our institutions. Sometimes the concerns are a response to individuals who use their institutional positions for selfish advantage. Sometimes the concerns are responses to the damage that institutions inflict on our social and natural environment. Sometimes the response is to the suffering that institutions impose on their own employees and managers. These concerns have led many to advocate the teaching of ethics to students who will enter these institutions and to employees and managers already in them. But what do these people need to learn?

Do they need to learn "how to behave"? Is it possible to teach that to people in organizations? Do they need to learn that they will get caught if they do not behave? But that approach will only touch a few. Both of these ideas, in fact, commit what might be called the *bad-apple fallacy,* which assumes that the bushel of apples is basically fine except for a few rotten ones. This fallacy oversimplifies the issue and serves as a smoke screen that prevents people from asking about the conditions of the whole bushel.

Some people argue that organizations need to learn to be responsible. But can responsibility be taught? I think it depends on what we mean by *responsibility.* If we mean *accountability,* then organizations can learn that they are accountable for their actions, but they usually learn this by government fines or consumer or employee lawsuits. Such ethical "lessons," however, have only limited value. They only provide organizations with information about what they cannot do. Although this ethical

1

approach to organizations is necessary at times, it does not really touch an organization's capacity to do what is right but rather only an organization's ability to do wrong. We need a broader definition of responsibility if we want to influence the heart of organizational life.

A contrast between positive and negative ethical guidelines can move us in this direction. A negative ethic only tells us what not to do: "Do not steal"; "Do not lie." A positive ethic, in contrast, gives us guidelines for what we should do. Instead of preventing harm, a positive ethic promotes the good. Most ethical systems contain both negative and positive guidelines, and so does the notion of responsibility. Negative responsibility refers to the obligation not to do harm. Corporations, for example, have a negative responsibility not to harm the natural environment, not to produce unsafe products, not to exploit workers, and so on. Positive responsibility, in contrast, would refer to a corporation's responsibility to do good such as to train and empower employees, to provide a good return on investment, to contribute to the development of society, and so forth. The positive meaning especially relies on the power of organizations to be responsive, to have the ability to respond. Organizations have abilities to respond to their members, to their society, and to the larger world. How to be responsible — to seriously consider how they should respond to issues they encounter — is something members of organizations can learn.

Remember the story about the hungry man? If you give a hungry man food, he will want more the next day. If you teach him to grow his own food, he will never be in want again. Ethics is like that. If you tell people what is right, you will have to tell them again tomorrow. If you teach them how to discover what is right, they will find the way themselves. At its best, ethics gives people a method, viable assumptions, and conceptual tools to decide that one course of action is more appropriate than another.

So, instead of seeing ethics as a set of rules or punishments, or even as a "code of ethics," we will define ethics as the process of deciding what should be done. These decisions may finally develop a code of ethics, but that is not really the goal.

The goal is to bring forth the resources so that people can make better decisions. Codes of conduct too easily become substitutes for ethical reflection. They may be helpful as guidelines or as partners in conversation, but when they take the place of the process, they stop the continuing conversation that keeps ethics alive.

The approach of this book draws on the understanding of responsibility as the ability to respond. It is based on the capacity of persons to weigh the pros and cons of different courses of action, to examine the reasons that support them, and to choose the course of action that has the most support. This approach sees ethics as a process of reflecting on the reasons for a proposed course of action. Through this process, participants can bring forth the resources essential for making the best decisions. This type of ethics does not provide answers but rather gives people the possibility of asking better questions and discovering the answers themselves. It gives an organization's members the conceptual tools and the communicative strategies to act responsibly.

For members of organizations to act responsibly, they need to take seriously at least three elements of organizational life: an organization's decision-making process, its systems of production and maintenance, and its culture. *Working Ethics* offers strategies and conceptual frameworks to analyze and improve the quality of all three. It demonstrates how the process of ethical reflection can bring forth valuable resources for making the right decisions, it develops an ethics of systems that shows how rights and justice can guide systems design, and it provides a strategy for analyzing assumptions. These contributions to organizational life will be briefly outlined here and then developed in the following chapters.

The Process of Ethical Reflection

A fundamental characteristic of organizations is their decision-making structure (Argyris and Schön, 1978; French, 1984; McCoy, 1985). Working within this structure, organizational members make decisions that affect not only their lives but also the lives of all of an organization's constituents — workers, consumers, investors, citizens, and so on. The process of ethical reflection can help make such decisions, because it enables decision makers to become aware of the value judgments and assumptions that implicitly operate throughout the decision-making process.

As will be demonstrated in Chapter Three, you cannot make a decision about what to do — a policy decision — without using value judgments and making assumptions. Unfortunately, because these aspects of the decision-making process are not as obvious as empirical data are, they are often ignored, even when they play a larger role in determining choices than all the data available. Ethical analysis helps decision makers understand, evaluate, and employ these elements of the process. Chapter Five provides some ethical criteria for such evaluations that have stood the test of time.

Discovering value judgments and evaluating them can create sharp disagreements in groups. Perhaps that is one reason people ignore value judgments as much as they do. In any case, for ethical analysis to really work in organizations, we need to learn how to handle disagreements. This will be addressed in Chapter Four and used as a theme throughout the book. Not having the skills to handle disagreements can result in ethical reflection that actually prevents a group from making decisions, as I learned from the following incident:

> A management consulting firm recently faced the question of whether to accept a project with a company that produced fuel for nuclear weapons. Some of the associates and support staff felt that they should take the project — what the company produced should not make any difference. Others believed that the production of nuclear arms was wrong, and they wanted to reject the contract. So the firm set up a conference to discuss what they should do. (I was invited as an "ethics consultant.")
>
> We developed an agenda with three parts:

information sharing, tools for analysis, and then discussion. I was in charge of the second part. I provided everyone with some concepts to use in assessing their relationships to work as well as to organizations. Everything went according to plan until we came to the discussion period.

After the discussion moved past the initial phase, the director of the firm asked that everyone simply share their opinions. For the next three hours, we went around the room, and twenty-five people shared the personal experiences that had moved them to accept or reject the proposal. After the sharing, the director asked for a hand count; about half of the group approved of the project and the other half disapproved, which closely resembled the division before the discussion began. Even though everyone said what they felt, and everyone listened to each other's stories with respect and understanding, the group itself had not really come any closer to a decision. So the executive committee later decided that each consultant could choose whether or not to work on the project.

The group certainly had taken up an important issue that required ethical reflection, if we understand ethics as the process of deciding what should be done. Their practice of ethical reflection, however, never really dealt with the disagreements within the group. It never attempted to show why one position was better than another or to analyze the strengths and weaknesses of the various positions. No one was ever challenged. Each member shared "where they were coming from," but members did not learn where the organization should be going. Although they learned to understand each other better, they did not increase their understanding of the project's strengths and weaknesses. They did not have the skills to challenge each other in a constructive manner and to deal effectively with disagreement. They lacked the communication skills and conceptual tools to engage in an effective analysis of the proposal.

In my work with people in organizations, I have developed an argumentative model of decision making that allows participants to handle disagreement, even to use disagreement as a resource for making better decisions. Once participants have discovered that arguing does not require fighting but rather can be an effective way to investigate the strengths and weaknesses of all proposals, they then can learn much more about the support of different positions than they knew before.

The process, which is covered in detail in Chapter Three, begins with the need to make a decision about a policy issue. It then analyzes the reasons for alternative courses of action, including the different data or observations about what is happening and the different value judgments and assumptions the participants use to support their positions. Finally, it leads the participants to examine the soundness of their agreements and disagreements and to select those that appear most persuasive to the group. In contrast to some decision-making processes, which begin with collecting data and then move toward proposals, this process begins with proposals and follows with a process of discovering the proposals' strengths and weaknesses. By beginning with proposals, participants can keep the discussion focused on the issue and the task at hand. Also, in many cases, participants already have some notion of what should be done. Stating possible options in the beginning enables the whole group to become aware of differences and preferences that might never come to light otherwise or only indirectly through unproductive quarreling over who has relevant information or authority. Beginning with differences, in other words, should enhance the process of discovering what can be done and what should be done. Sometimes, of course, when no one has any idea of what should be done, we need to collect information before we can ask the right questions. Argumentative analysis has its limits and may come into play only after the initial formulation of proposals. In many cases, however, decision makers come to meetings knowing what they want the group to decide and also knowing that others have different ideas. In such cases, argumentative analysis can be a very effective way to arrive at a group decision. This process does not guarantee that the group will make the right decision, but it does guarantee that the decision will be responsible—that is, that the participants have made the best decision given their resources.

For argumentative analysis to work, members must know that their views will be taken seriously and that the analysis will focus on the strengths and weaknesses of their arguments rather than on their character. All participants must be protected from personal attack and be challenged to discover reasons for all views. For differences to become productive, participants need to overcome any tendency to become defensive and avoid conflict and need to become mutually engaged in an open inquiry into the materials that all members contribute to the discussion.

People argue not only about value judgments and assumptions but also about information, and I have found that some skill in analyzing generalizations, cause-and-effect relations, relations between parts and whole, and comparisons and contrasts helps participants to raise questions when they doubt the facts presented but do not know how best to express their doubts. Chapter Six contains several effective ways to evaluate factual statements. The process of ethical reflection includes consideration of observations, value judgments, and assumptions as well as the way these can be used together to develop strong reasons for a proposed course of action. This process can help decision makers at all levels of an organization to make better decisions.

When groups have reached a decision, a good question to ask is "Now what?" The answer, especially in organizations, requires that we look at the organization's system, because in many cases good decisions will only be implemented if they are somehow compatible with the organization's system. If they do not fit, then the system itself must be changed before people can do what they have decided is right. Because of the importance of an organization's system for carrying out the results of ethical reflection, and because an organization's system determines whether resources are distributed fairly, responsible organizations need to develop an ethics of systems to guide their design and management.

The Ethics of Systems

We can understand much about the nature of systems by examining the sport of basketball. Like most games, basketball has both written and unwritten rules. One unwritten rule is that you should steal the ball from the other team whenever you can as long as you do not break any written rule. If one player believes it is wrong to steal the ball and refuses to, then this player punishes his or her whole team. If you want to stop players from stealing, you have to change the way everyone plays the game. They have the right to steal the ball in the current system of basketball. If an individual believes that that is wrong, he or she must change the rules of the game or quit playing. Sometimes, of course, new rules are instituted, primarily for one of three reasons: to protect individuals, to make the game more fair, or to ensure that the game remains interesting and energizing. These three reasons apply not only to basketball but to other human systems as well. Human systems must recognize the rights of their members, they must be fair or just, and they must be energetic, or, to use another term, they must generate *power*. To develop a responsible organization, we need to understand its generation and use of power, the kind of justice it should practice, and the individual rights it should respect. If a system is just and rights are respected, groups will have the power to do what is right.

In past decades, the various constituencies of organizations have given voice to their rights. Workers speak of the rights to organize, to equal pay for equal work, to equal opportunity, to fairness, to strike, to training, to due process, and to safe work conditions. Consumers speak of the rights to safe products, to honest dealings, to information, and to due care. Citizens speak of the rights to a safe and clean environment, to constrain land use, to controlled growth, and to economic stability. Investors speak of the rights to profits, to effective management, and to fiduciary responsibility. Corporations claim the rights to do business, to hire and fire, and to monitor employees. The exclusive emphasis on rights, however, has tended to ignore the organizational systems within which rights make their claims.

It also tends to ignore the necessity of examining the system and particularly how the system distributes its power. In other words, they ignore the importance of an organization's practice of internal and external justice. The importance of justice for organizations has been clearly formulated by John Rawls: "Justice is the first virtue of social institutions, as truth is of systems of thought. A theory however elegant and economical must be rejected or revised if it is untrue; likewise laws and institutions no matter how efficient and well-arranged must be reformed or abolished if they are unjust" (1971, p. 3). Acknowledging the significance of justice still does not answer the question of what kind of justice organizations should practice. Organizations clearly do not practice equal justice. In fact, an organizational structure dictates a vast array of "inequalities." How can these inequalities be justified? Some strategies for answering this question will be presented in Chapter Eight.

An organization, of course, is not only a network of power relations but also a network of persons. On the one hand, organizations structure relationships to accomplish some organizational goals. Offices, positions, job descriptions, and organizational charts outline the structure of an organization's system. On the other hand, an organization is also a company of persons, and their interaction throughout the work environment signals so much more than what exists on paper — on organizational charts. Put simply, organizations organize human beings. They are both systems and communities. People speak and act, listen and react, respond or withdraw. An ethics of systems needs to consider how the organization's system affects the organization's human community, especially in terms of human rights and organizational justice.

As human communities, organizations become places where persons make themselves into something as they also make something for the organization. It is the place to "make a living," in the double sense of gaining the means necessary for life and of developing the meaning of life. Because organizations are human communities, members ask questions not only about their survival but also about their human rights and social justice. How we think justice should be practiced in organizations, or what it actually means to respect persons' rights, depends not only on our understanding of these ethical criteria but also on our assumptions about how things work in organizations and, more generally, our assumptions about ourselves and others. So an ethics of systems, like the process of ethical reflection, finally requires a method to analyze basic assumptions. This brings us to our third concern — an organization's and its members' basic assumptions.

Analyzing Assumptions

The notion of *assumptions* refers to what Alfred Schutz has called the "life-world," which he defines as follows: "By the everyday life-world is to be understood that province of reality which the wide awake and normal adult simply takes for granted in the attitude of common sense. By this taken-for-grantedness, we designate everything that we experience as unquestionable; every state of affairs is for us unproblematic until further notice" (1973, p. 3).

Edgar Schein has given a similar definition for an organization's culture when he defines it as those "*basic assumptions* and *beliefs* that are shared by members of an organization, that operate unconsciously, and that define in a basic 'taken-for-granted' fashion an organization's view of itself and its environment" (italics his) (1985, p. 6). Given this understanding of culture, as taken-for-granted or unconscious assumptions, it would be almost impossible to analyze assumptions in a completely homogeneous or monolithic society. We would have few opportunities to become conscious of our assumptions. In our pluralistic and changing society, however, we continually find ourselves confronted with outdated or dysfunctional assumptions, and in some cases we move from what has been "common sense" to what makes "good sense."

Many of us have discovered that we live in subcultures instead of in a single unifying culture. We speak of the Jewish culture, the Anglo-Saxon Protestant culture, African-American and Hispanic cultures, and male and female cultures. As Schein shows in his analysis of organizational cultures, different organizations also can have very different cultures. Most organizations have different subcultures as well. At least, their different stakeholders will have different assumptions about the organization (Mason and Mitroff, 1981). The presence of subcultures gives us the possibility of reflecting on our own taken-for-granted assumptions and evaluating their appropriateness in particular situations, their relevance to actual possibilities, and their coherence with our actions and aspirations. These possibilities remain difficult to realize, however, because assumptions serve as the underpinning for our interpretations of reality. Still, it is possible, and perhaps inevitable, for our assumptions to change as we discover other underpinnings that seem to work better.

The types of assumptions that have particular relevance for ethical reflection are those that Schutz sees as determined by a "pragmatic motive" (1973, p. 6). We could call these assumptions implicit knowledge of how to get something done or assumptions about "how things work." Two groups, for example, may use justice as a value judgment, and yet one group may promote justice by developing rules and another group by promoting social interaction. Even though the groups have the same value, they have different assumptions about how justice becomes a reality. Chapter Nine will show how to further analyze this and other assumptions.

This book relies on the basic assumption that people can discuss what should be done in organizations. On one level, of course, communication is necessary for the maintenance of any organization. On another level, the kind of discussion that ethical reflection requires should not be taken for granted. If organizations are to engage in ethical reflection as a means of increasing their ability to respond—their responsibility—then they must develop a culture where doing ethical analysis of their decision-making process is not only good sense but also common sense.

In the following chapters, you will have opportunities to engage in ethical reflection and analysis. Chapter Two begins with a description of the ethical perspective, which shows how ethics itself interprets human action and organizations. This chapter sets the primary framework for the rest of the book. Chapter Three outlines and shows how to use the five resources for ethical reflection — policy proposals, observations, value judgments, assumptions, and opposing views — to discover the right decision. The argumentative model developed in Chapter Three allows groups to examine each aspect of the process and the relationships between them. Chapters Four, Five, and Six present strategies and concepts to handle differences in policy proposals, value judgments, and observations. After learning how to use these resources, groups should have adequate materials to engage in productive ethical reflection on organizational policy questions.

Chapter Seven moves to our second major concern: an ethics of systems. It presents a systems approach to organizations and analyzes the connections between systems and power. Because neither systems nor power have their own guidance systems, Chapter Eight turns to the notions of rights and justice as a way of determining what inequalities can be justified in organizations. Chapter Nine addresses the question of basic assumptions and shows how to analyze the relationship between assumptions and value judgments in organizational life. It also examines some assumptions about organizational life and about how things work in organizations. The alternatives developed should enable readers to examine their own assumptions. Chapter Ten then turns to our assumptions about communication in organizations, since these assumptions will determine whether or not people engage in ethical reflections at work. Chapter Eleven brings together much that has been presented in the book by first describing some of the conditions necessary for ethics to work in organizations and then providing some plans for training people in the process of ethical reflection. The worksheets in Chapter Eleven, referenced throughout the book, may be helpful as you proceed. They can also be used as material for training groups.

Chapter Two

Developing an Ethical Perspective

Faced with a reduction in its projection income for the next year, management sent a memo to the various department heads to cut their expenses by 20 percent. The memo also stated that department heads could decide whether to include their staff in the decision of how to make the cut.

The head of the finance department, Jill Wong, thought about the costs and benefits of including the whole department. On the one hand, she thought it would benefit the department if staff participation increased morale. On the other hand, it would cost the department work time and maybe even prevent them from meeting their deadlines. Also, the staff might develop an alternative unacceptable to management — a potential cost. Jill considered the costs and benefits of involving the staff because her decision depended on which one outweighed the other.

In the human resource department, Ray Jones was thinking in a different direction. He thought that empowering his staff would increase the quality of their work. Letting the staff participate would also increase job satisfaction and let the staff feel like they "owned" the decision. He also knew he had a pattern of not respecting or expressing his own power. Maybe this time he should use it instead of giving it away. Instead of looking at the costs and benefits, Ray evaluated the effect of the decision on self-esteem and personal growth.

If we review how Jill and Ray thought about their choices, it is clear that Jill used an economic perspective and Ray used a psychological perspective. Managers in other departments could give other interpretations of the situation, depending on their perspective. Their perspective depends on their training, their subgroup, and their personal and social life.

Most of us have become accustomed to the presentation of various perspectives. During the media coverage of the 1989 Loma Prieta earthquake in Northern California, for example, we learned about its likely political, economic, and psychological consequences. The same event was interpreted in different ways, from different perspectives, and each interpretation increased our understanding of the full consequences of the earthquake. Another perspective, and the one that interests us here, is the ethical perspective. To engage successfully in ethical reflection, we need a perspective that will bring into view the moral dimensions of organizational life.

One distinguishing character of a perspective is its language. When you begin to use a particular language, you also begin to select those aspects of a situation that the language names. Talk like an economist, and you see things economically. Talk like a psychologist, and you see psychologically. Furthermore, using a particular language leads you to ask the kinds of questions that you can answer in that language. The question "What are the costs and benefits" opens the possibility for economic answers. The question "What levels of needs will this policy fulfill?" opens the possibility for psychological answers.

The questions that an ethical perspective encourages us to ask bring to mind some things that other perspectives overlook. For example, the ethical question "Am I being responsible to others?" can bring into view the obligations that we have toward each other. The language of responsibility, of course, represents only a fraction of the language of ethics. The discipline of ethics brings with it a rich tradition of interpretation and a variety of approaches for interpreting human conduct. Each approach configures the situation in a special fashion, allowing us to see some things that we probably have not seen before.

Even though speaking a particular vocabulary is necessary for taking up a perspective, it is not a guarantee of attaining that perspective. Words can become separated from their original outlook on the world, and people can then employ them freely. This happens all the time. The word *interface* is a good example. At one time *interface* was primarily used in conjunction with computers, but now even people are "interfacing" with each other. When words become disconnected from their context, they easily become stray pieces of jargon, sounding important but not telling us very much. Do you know what people do when they "interface"? We forget that words belong not only to thought but also to a world (Gusdorf, 1965, pp. 42–43). Words belong to a world because they articulate or formulate the world in a particular way. They put it in perspective.

Actually, words have both a connotative and a denotative meaning. The denotative meaning invokes a particular interpretation of situations. It is the word's reference to the world. The connotative meaning belongs to the word itself. It is the emotive meaning that the word provokes. Ethical language, unfortunately, appears particularly susceptible to losing its denotative meaning—its reference to particular actions and attitudes—and being abused by its connotative meaning—its emotional meaning. Recently, for example, a California corporation gave the title "ethical guidelines" to its old list of rules and regulations for employees. Using ethical language like this is a kind of "word magic," signifying nothing. Employees knew nothing had changed in their real world of work. If ethics is going to work in organizations, and if people are to be prevented from exploiting ethics for their own benefit, it is necessary to keep track of the denotative meaning of ethical language, and we do that by taking up the ethical perspective.

The term *responsible,* for example, has a positive connotative meaning, but it can easily become mere jargon if it does not also reveal something about the real world. What is the denotative meaning of *responsibility?* Does it not reveal a world of human action, of persons and organizations having power—the capacity to respond? Does it not also show persons as actors who care about their acts' consequences for others? The word reveals a particular world and assumes a particular way of looking at things—an ethical perspective.

Ethics assumes that people have the freedom and power to respond—that is, the freedom and power to consider different options, to analyze the options' strengths and weaknesses, and to choose one option over the others based on its merits. These assumptions provide a way of looking at situations and of responding to the various parties involved. Assumptions can be further refined by examining some of the chief characteristics of an ethical perspective of human conduct. An ethical perspective focuses on action rather than behavior, it looks for reasons that justify acts rather than explain behavior, and it acknowledges the gap between "ought" and "is."

Ethics Focuses on Action Rather Than Behavior

I know that ethics has been associated with good behavior, but I want to show that this emphasis betrays the real power of ethical reflection and that it actually does not belong to an ethical perspective of human conduct. The difference between behavior and action can be illustrated by the differences in these two sentences:

Congress behaved well.
Congress acted well.

Does not the first refer more to etiquette or perhaps to a negative ethics of not doing anything wrong—the members stayed out of trouble—while the second refers to the members enacting the right legislation? Even when behaving well has the connotation of moral conduct, its denotative meaning refers more to conforming to rules than to using one's power (ability) to make an appropriate response.

The term *behavior* has also become entangled in the theory of psychological behaviorism, and this notion of behavior is even further removed from ethical responsibility (Nye, 1975). According to behaviorism, people do not act but only react. Their social conditioning determines their response to external stimuli; to change the response, you merely change the stimuli. Through positive and negative reinforcement, you can even have them do what is right. Such a "well-behaved" person does what is right, however, because of prior conditioning rather than because of his or her decision. In contrast to the behaviorist, who assumes that people act as they do because of their pattern of reactions, an ethicist assumes that people act because they decided it was the right thing to do. In other words, actors choose not only because of their past experience or even because of their values—behaviorists talk about values, too—but also because at that particular time they decide in favor of one particular possibility rather than another.

Behaviorism does partially fit our everyday understanding of conduct. We think of a well-behaved person as someone who automatically does the right thing because of proper training. In some situations, of course, such as driving a car, proper training is essential. We need to act almost instinctively and just as predictably and as quickly as a dog will respond to a bell. When ethical language is used as a "bell" for employee conduct, though, ethics has forfeited its real potential to promote organizational responsibility.

When you consider whether to accept the theory of behaviorism, an inconsistency immediately becomes apparent: How can you wonder whether to accept a theory that denies such choices? This inconsistency can be seen in Gullett and Reisen's appeal for managers to become committed to behavior modification: "Finally, we need to convince ourselves of the value and utility of the operant approach to motivation. It has proven its usefulness, but it can only succeed if we study it, understand it, and have the courage to apply it" (1980, p. 219). The decisions to study and to understand, and especially the courage to apply, certainly cannot be accounted for by behaviorism. Such inconsistencies occur whenever people take up a perspective toward others that differs from how they see themselves.

Because people can use ethical language to control behavior by pressuring others to submit to ethical rules or they can use ethical language to empower others by engaging them in the process of ethical reflection, we need to fully grasp the perspective that ethical analysis requires. If we are to achieve the necessary alignment between what we say and what we see, then we need to develop a perspective of human conduct that assumes that people will do more than simply behave and that they will also consider and act on their best judgment. When we are looking at human conduct, we look for responsible action rather than conditioned behavior. When we ask about the reasons for such action, we look for a justification rather than an explanation — our second refinement of the ethical perspective.

Ethics Justifies Action Rather Than Explaining Behavior

Suppose someone continually comes in late for work, and you ask for a reason. You can receive two different kinds of answers: an explanation or a justification. An explanation will demonstrate what caused such behavior. You may hear about poor time management, lack of adequate child care, or other causes for this behavior. Such an explanation differs sharply from an employee's possible justification. Even though we sometimes use the term *justification* to mean a rationalization or even an excuse for doing something, its basic meaning is quite different. To justify, according to the *Random House Dictionary of the English Language* (1971, p. 776), is "to show (an act, claim, statement, etc.) to be just, right, or warranted." Whereas an explanation will show what caused an action, a justification will show what principles or values the actor used in making his or her choice. For example, if the employee who was late tried to justify the behavior, this would be done with reference to particular standards of conduct or principles — say, the idea that parental obligations take precedence over one's job.

Although the contrast between explanation and justification usually applies in adult life, when we look for the reasons behind a child's conduct, the distinction becomes blurred. For example, you could explain why a child left his or her parents by showing stages of growth and so on. But if you see the child as making a choice — acting rather than merely behaving — then you acknowledge the child's power to choose one alternative rather than another. Both interpretations can be valid. They are really complementary; they are also different.

Our legal system provides another interesting illustration of this distinction. In defending a suspected murderer, the defense may try to show that the defendant did not choose to kill the victim but was moved to do it. Psychological and sociological explanations may show that the defendant had no choice in the matter—it just happened. The defendant, in other words, is not responsible for his or her conduct (the defendant did not have the ability to respond). The use of these defenses, even when they are convincing, as they sometimes are, should not blind us to the basic assumption of our legal system—namely, that people are responsible for their conduct. Justice assumes we have the ability to respond.

Psychological and sociological interpretations of most of our conduct, both as individuals and as groups, can be very persuasive. In many cases, we discover that what we thought we had freely chosen turns out to have been largely caused by our early family or cultural history. Choice always occurs within the thick context of our entire life, most of which we did not choose. At the same time, we also must decide what we will do. To justify our decisions in these cases, we go beyond what we have already done to what we ought to do. Even within the given context of our lives, we do have some choices about what we ought to do.

Ethics Acknowledges the Gap Between "Ought" and "Is"

Modern philosophical ethics rests on the assumption that you cannot decide what you ought to do from what is. To make such a decision commits the "naturalistic fallacy"—the fallacy of assuming that just because something is, it should be. G. E. Moore argues this point in reference to evolutionist ethics: "These doctrines are those which maintain that the course of 'evolution,' while it shews us the direction in which we *are* developing, thereby and for that reason shews us the direction in which we *ought* to develop" ([1903] 1978, p. 46). This kind of reasoning commits the naturalistic fallacy. In other words, to say that evolution is good entails the judgment that we ought to consider it good. Actually, we asssume the distinction between "is" and "ought" all the time. We know that although everyone is

doing something, it could still be wrong. What people or organizations do cannot tell us what they ought to do. If we cannot
find out what we ought to do from what is, where can we find
it? We find it in our values, beliefs, and principles, for example, the principles of fairness and human dignity. Instead of
finding support for our decision by explaining what moved us
to make it or by referring to what others have done — they could
be wrong — we support it by supplying principles or other ethical criteria that serve as justifications for the decision.

The distinction between "is" and "ought" parallels, in many
ways, a distinction between descriptive and normative ethics.
Descriptive ethics describes how people do act and explains their
action in terms of their value judgments and assumptions.
Prescriptive or normative ethics studies how people ought to
act and analyzes the value judgments and assumptions that
would justify such actions. While descriptive ethics increases
our understanding of ourselves and others and thereby our understanding of right conduct, we still must choose how we ought
to act and determine how we can justify such choices. These
choices rely on our value judgments and ultimately our assumptions. The differences between descriptive and normative ethics
parallel the other differences we have reviewed, as the following list shows.

Descriptive ethics	Normative ethics
What is	What ought to be
Explanation	Justification
Behavior	Action

These columns represent two paths for ethical reflection, and
even though the path of normative ethics is the one less often
taken, it alone has the potential to enable organizational responsibility. The normative path, however, is only a path for discovering our value judgments, not for discovering our basic assumptions. The following example will help to explain the difference
between value judgments and assumptions.

Rosalee Peterson decides to continue her education by
obtaining a master's degree. Her reasons are that people with

advanced degrees have a better chance for promotion in her company and that she wants a promotion. The first reason describes a current practice. It does not tell us what Rosalee should do but only what is happening. The second reason indirectly indicates what Rosalee values, which we could translate into the belief that she thinks she should develop her potential or increase her standard of living. These values could justify her decision. If we then question these values, we move toward Rosalee's assumptions. She assumes, let us say, that people should realize their own potential because "we are born to become the best that we can be." Or she may assume that if you do not take advantage of opportunities when they come, they might never come again. These assumptions indicate her beliefs about what is rather than what ought to be. They also serve as the basis for Rosalee's decision to continue her education. Such beliefs express our assumptions about reality — about what is. They bring into our perspective, at a different level than observations, the dimension of the "is."

Here is another example of how our assumptions about reality work in ethical reflection. Some people believe that workers have a right to know their company's goals, because it increases workers' ability to have control over their own lives. The right to control one's own life, then, justifies their position. If this principle is questioned, we need to develop a further justification that supports the principle. Why should individuals and groups have control over their own lives? We could say, "Because exercising control increases moral responsibility, and moral responsibility is a necessary aspect of human maturity." This statement refers to our basic understanding about a mature person's character. How do we know that the statement is true? Our only answer is that we are the kind of beings who have the capacity for moral responsibility, who expect moral responsibility of others, who live in a tradition of moral responsibility, and who have continually passed the tradition on to the next generation. It is not just that we *ought to be* morally responsible but rather that fundamentally we *are*. What we are, however, refers not to what we observe (we certainly observe irresponsible conduct) but to what we assume about the nature of human beings. In other words, when we investigate the ultimate basis for our "oughts," we find our understanding of reality—our basic assumptions about what is.

Our basic assumptions dissolve any absolute distinction between "is" and "ought" and complicate the relationship between the two. Instead of just two concepts—"is" and "ought"—we have a third concept that connects them: our basic assumptions about reality. These basic assumptions, after all, provide the ultimate support for our ethical perspective. The basic assumptions that set forth the necessary framework for ethical analysis are that persons are moral agents and that organizations are moral communities and moral agents.

Persons as Moral Agents

Moral agents are persons who can consider alternative courses of action and can justify their choice with good reasons. To take up an ethical perspective toward one another—toward our co-workers—means to attribute this power to them. The other implication of the power to choose, of course, is responsibility for the choice. People can be held accountable for their actions. Some individuals may not possess or may even lose their power of choice and therefore accountability. For example, the "diminished capacity" legal plea tries to show that defendants—at the time of their act—could not tell right from wrong and did not have the ability to choose. From an ethical perspective, the intent in such cases is to show that these individuals should not be seen as moral agents.

We do not attribute moral agency to infants and young children, either. Although they generally have the potential to become moral agents, they do not yet have the capacity to exercise moral judgment. That is why we have juvenile courts. When people become moral agents is a subject of debate, and the issues are very complicated. People may have power and accountability at an early age in some situations but not in others. To approach very small children as though they were morally competent surely misses the mark. Some human activities simply should not be interpreted morally or ethically—

interpreted in terms of right and wrong or good and bad. Because we are primarily concerned with the practice of ethics in adult organizations, we can assume moral agency until we are surprised by its absence.

So, our first basic assumption is that members of organizations — our co-workers — are moral agents. In contrast to a behaviorist perspective, which may try to manipulate the behavior of others through reward and punishment systems or through modern techniques of behavior modification, an ethical perspective looks at others as willful, powerful individuals. If Jill and Ray used an ethical perspective, do you think they would choose to include their co-workers in solving the problem of how to deal with the budget cut? From an ethical perspective, their perception of their staffs' moral agency — their power and freedom to choose the right thing to do — may well mean that they will choose to include their co-workers. Jill and Ray will also need to consider the impact of their decision on the organization's moral community.

Organizations as Moral Communities

Because of the extensive and sometimes vague use of the term *community,* we need to use this term with care. Few books in business or organizational ethics have used the term, although there are some exceptions (McCoy, 1985). Our concern, of course, is not whether we observe organizations as communities but whether it is realistic to assume that organizations are communities, despite some appearances to the contrary. The reluctance to use the term *community* may come from the anonymity of large corporations. If they are communities, then they are certainly "communities of strangers." It is simply impossible for thousands of organizational members to really know each other, which seems like a main characteristic of any real community. The need to know each other, however, may not be the best criterion for determining the presence of community. In any case, if we are to interpret organizations as communities, then we will need to justify the notion of a "public community" where people can remain strangers, in the sense of not knowing much about each other's private lives, and yet at the same time are able to acknowledge that each other's well-being is bound up with the well-being of the organization as a whole. Community, in other words, is some form of solidarity.

In contrast to mass culture, which is composed of isolated and anonymous individuals, a communal culture is based on the interplay between individual and communal interests. In a community, one finds an interdependence between communal maturity and individual maturity. We live in different communities, of course, including family, neighborhood, and religious communities, and they have different meanings for us. Although people have sometimes seen the workplace as a substitute for more traditional communities, it stretches the imagination to call an organization—especially a large corporation—a family. At the same time, because organizations are networks of human interaction, they can be considered to be one type of community among others. We certainly expect different things from these communities, but in every community the dynamic of self-development and community development remains interdependent. Although in different ways in different communities, "we are largely formed by the communities of what we are a part, and through our actions, which shape our communities, we influence the development of ourselves and of others" (Kammer, 1988, p. 141).

Some people may agree to a community of workers and a community of managers or owners but reject the notion of corporate community. This position overlooks the interdependence of these two groups. Solidarity does not mean a lack of conflict or disagreement, but it does mean some overriding unity that holds conflicts and disagreements together. The history of industrialization certainly reveals times when managers and workers did not share any such unity, but should we interpret this as the normal state of affairs or as a disruption of an organization's basic community? As I will argue in Chapter Eight when I discuss justice and rights, human rights ultimately belong to all who are members of the human community, and the justice of this community determines whether people will enjoy the rights to which they are entitled. Ethical analysis is not singing in the dark here; it is exposing the basic assumptions that finally make human life human.

To speak of an organization as a "moral community" allows us to acknowledge the moral significance of human interaction and relations within organizations. It brings forth for thought the bonds or relationships that unite community members. The type and structure of these bonds, of course, may differ in different communities, and members may be united as allies or as adversaries. Community does not mean absence of conflict but rather conflict among members. Even in conflict, whatever holds the community together serves as the foundation for its moral character. The question is not whether an organization is a moral community but rather what kind of moral community it is.

Organizations as Moral Agents

To view organizations, and especially business corporations, as moral agents assumes they are responsible for what they do. Is this a plausible assumption? Perhaps it is more appropriate to use a behaviorist perspective. Some people like to believe that, like small children or animals, corporations merely react to external stimuli — for example, public opinion, market conditions, and consumer preferences — and really do not consider what is right or wrong. However, this seems more like an interpretation of what some corporations do than an interpretation of what they should do. To think about what corporations should do, we need to understand what it means to call them moral agents. As previously stated, moral agency involves the ability to consider alternative courses of action, to choose one course rather than another, and to justify the decision by appealing to appropriate standards of conduct. Can corporations do this? This question has caused a good deal of debate, and we can discover what it means to speak of organizations as moral agents by examining some of the arguments.

Let us use the 1989 Valdez oil spill tragedy in Alaska as a case to help us understand the different positions on moral agency. One position is that only, or at least primarily, individuals are responsible for acts. Manuel Velasquez, for example, argues that only individuals really make decisions and act. He thinks that to call their acts "corporate acts" is only a linguistic convention (1988, p. 21). On the one hand, it is true that corporations are "legal fictions," which means that their legal status depends on the law and not on their actual existence. In a sense, corporations exist only at the pleasure of the governments who grant them their status. It is always possible for the people, through their representative government, to dissolve corporations. As Chapter Eight will demonstrate, although corporations have some of the same legal or civil rights as human beings, they do not share the same human rights. Therefore, it does make sense to distinguish between humans and corporations.

In the Valdez case, many individuals were responsible. Those directly involved had some responsibility. It seems that the ship captain acted irresponsibly by drinking, as did some members of the crew by tolerating his conduct, as did those who had reports of his past conduct and allowed him to stay in his position. You could also ask if the people who sold alcohol to the crew were responsible. These people had choices and are responsible for them. Corporate management also had choices. They could have developed and implemented policies that would have created a more responsible work force. They could have decided to use tankers with a double lining that would have withstood the blow the tanker suffered. They could have decided to operate only when the emergency equipment was fully in place. So, individuals were certainly responsible. If only individuals were responsible, however, then why should they not be required to do the cleanup? Since Exxon was required to do the cleanup, perhaps the corporation was responsible also. To see how it could be responsible, we need to look at how corporate decisions are made.

In describing the decision-making process in corporations, Peter French argues that we should attribute moral agency to them. In his *Collective and Corporate Responsibility,* French begins his explanation by drawing a distinction between crowds and corporations (1984, p. 19). Crowds, he contends, are simply aggregates of individuals, whereas corporations are decision-making systems that give to corporations the characteristics of a moral person. French uses the term *person* not as a reference to ourselves as humans but rather as a reference to ourselves as intentional actors. A person, in his view, denotes intentionality and rationality. So, to treat a corporation as a moral person, we must be able to describe what a corporation does as "intended by the corporation itself" (1984, p. 39). French explains that an organization's "Corporate Internal Decision [CID] structure" gives intentions to an organization. The three elements of the CID structure are the flowchart or organizational chart, procedural rules, and corporate policies. As decisions are processed through these structures, they become corporate decisions. "Simply, when the corporation act is consistent with an instantiation or an implementation of established corporate policy, then it is proper to describe it as having been done for corporate reasons, as having been caused by a corporate desire coupled with a corporate belief and so, in other words, as corporate intentional" (1984, p. 44).

While French interprets corporations as having intentions and therefore moral agency, Velasquez argues that only human persons have intentions. Velasquez (1983) sees intentions as referring to both mental and bodily movements, and since corporations do not have a human body, they cannot have intentions. Perhaps we can resolve this difference by making a distinction between motive and intention. *Motive* would refer to a person's "motivation" or more subjective reasons for acting. *Intention* can refer, then, to choosing a particular act. For example, I could be motivated by a concern for quality to talk to a co-worker about his or her sloppy work. I could also be motivated by anger. This motivation, however, would differ from what I intend to do — to talk to my co-worker. I could also express my concern by talking to my supervisor. If this distinction makes sense, then we could say that corporations do not have motives, but they do have intentions, as French suggests.

Still, to call a corporation a moral person does seem odd. If we remember that the term *person* originally meant *persona,* or a mask that actors wore in Greek drama, we could use the term to "mask" any decision-making process. We usually use the term, however, in the sense of *personal,* which denotes the subjectivity of human existence. Corporations do not possess this kind of subjectivity. As Velasquez says, corporations do not feel pleasure or pain (1988, p. 20). Thus to call corporations moral persons seems unlikely to correspond with our normal use of the term. A better term would be simply *moral agent* or *moral agency.* Charles McCoy, for example, uses moral agency in his analysis of corporate decision making: "Corporate moral agency does not consist of adherence to a list of ideal norms. Instead, corporate moral agency refers to that process of choosing certain goals rather than others, selecting means for attaining them, setting standards of performance, guiding implementation, and evaluating results" (1985, p. 72). By affirming the moral agency of organizations, we can attribute to them the same characteristics as we do to human moral agents — power to make choices and responsibility for them.

Returning to the Valdez case, the notion of corporate moral agency does help us understand why Exxon is also responsible. Exxon's policies about employee accountability, about the kinds of ships to use, and about safety requirements were developed through the corporate decision-making structures, and were made for corporate reasons. Here, we can say that both individuals and corporations can be viewed as moral agents. Some of these decisions — such as to use only safe tankers — need to take into account the problems of international competition and therefore require a systems approach, which we will discuss in Chapter Seven. As we will see, participants in systems are also responsible for their design. Exxon may also be held responsible under the rule of strict liability. Strict liability means that no matter who is at fault, the actor must repair any damage. It is something like borrowing someone's automobile. People expect that when it is returned, it will be in the same condition as before. Likewise, communities may expect that whenever corporations "borrow" natural resources for their business, they will make sure that they return the resources to their prior condition. In such cases, corporations become responsible even for accidental damage, because they have chosen to take the risk. This choice makes them responsible.

Once we recognize that both individuals and corporations are moral agents, we need to know how they are related to each other. Larry May thinks we should view individuals as "vicariously" acting for the organization: "'Acting vicariously' means that one person acts in behalf of another, or conversely an entity acts through a person whose action is then re-described as the action of the entity" (1987, p. 51). The notion of vicarious action keeps us from forgetting that corporations cannot act by themselves. If no one shows up for work, the organization cannot act. I think that most would agree with May's view that an organization "is not a specific entity that acts, but a process through which actions occur" (1987, p. 43). During that process sometimes individuals will decide in favor of acts that they would also have chosen for themselves; in other cases, they will support decisions that they would not have made for themselves but that were the best decisions for the corporation. These individuals will justify their decision by the corporation's mission and standards of conduct and not by their own. What is good for the corporation, as well as what is good for them as individuals, will finally be determined by their choices. Since the whole process is characterized by choices involving the corporation's mission and policies as well as choices of how to design the process and whom to involve, the corporation can be considered a moral agent. To explore what choices an organization has when faced with a particular issue, you can use the worksheet, shown in Exhibit 2 in Chapter Eleven, that asks for the decision, the options, and the reason one option was selected.

The process of making such a choice deserves all the resources it can muster so that the choice is right. This process can profit from ethical reflection, because, as we will see in the next chapter, the process of ethical reflection increases the resources for making decisions about what should be done. The process of ethical reflection depends on people taking an ethical perspective toward human action and organizations. Without this perspective, ethical reflection can too easily lose its own integrity and become an instrument for any number of purposes.

Chapter Three

Discovering the Right Decision

Our reflections follow the path of our questions. Ethical reflection begins when we question a policy or action proposal. It follows the way opened by questions such as: "What should we do?" "What do we know?" "What does it mean?" "Why does it mean that?" We do not always ask these questions when we face decisions. Sometimes we simply act, and our action counts as a decision. At other times, even though we recognize different possible courses of action, we choose without giving reasons for the choice. If others disagree, they do so in silence. In some cases, however, not only do we face alternative choices, but people present different versions of what is happening and evaluate it differently. In such cases, before a group can come to a decision, it needs to investigate these differences. The *process of ethical reflection* refers to this type of analysis.

Suppose you are a member of a group faced with a decision about what the group should do. You may have an idea, but the group has not yet reached a consensus or even discussed all the options. You do not even know if everyone has the same information or a similar sense of the importance of what is happening. Your best guess, however, is that people have different ideas about what should be done. Given this situation and assuming the proper conditions for open discussions, you can take several steps to engage the group in a conversation about what to do.

The first step involves gathering the relevant resources for making the decision. *Resources* here refers to the means that groups have to discover the right decision. The means include first of all the participants' policy proposals and their data or observations. These initial resources entail two other resources: value judgments and basic assumptions. Once the discussion begins, the participants discover a fifth resource: opposing views. Once these five resources have been identified, then the group can take the next steps of evaluating and using them to analyze the strengths and weaknesses of different courses of action. As groups develop their ability to use these resources, they also develop another significant resource: the means to engage in ethical reflection.

Five Resources for Making Decisions

Enabling a group decision requires a different set of resources than we might use for just ourselves. When making individual decisions, we may rely on intuition, experience, feelings, or external authority. When others in a group have different intuitions, experiences, feelings, or authorities, these resources usually confound rather than promote the decision-making process. When Greg says, "But I just can't do that, because it does not feel right," and Tim says, "But I feel all right about it," there is not much more they can say. Although feelings give us important clues about issues, they seldom lead to productive discussions with people who verbalize different feelings. For example, I may feel very strongly that corporations should provide child care, but if I express only my feelings, then people who do not share them will probably not be persuaded. If I justify these feelings, however, by talking about the proper relationship between work and family life or the benefits of such programs for all concerned, then others may not only agree that my feelings make sense, but also that changes should be made. In other words, we need to give reasons that others can investigate and reflect on. The four questions of ethical reflection will bring forth the following resources:

Question	Resource
What should we do?	People's policy proposals
What do we know?	Their observations
What does it mean?	Their value judgments
Why does it mean that?	Their basic assumptions

These four resources — proposals, observations, value
judgments, and basic assumptions — all belong to the decision-
making process, even if we do not always sort them out so neatly
in our everyday work. The fifth resource, opposing views, offers
another view of the appropriate selection and use of these four
resources. To see the steps in using the resources for making
decisions, we can place them on a decision-making diamond,
as shown in Figure 1.

Figure 1.

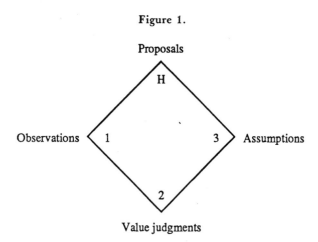

We start at home plate (H). Someone pitches us a policy
question, such as "Should we cut back on our employee assistance
program?" We propose a course of action and see if everyone
agrees. If they do, then we simply act — a home run. If they do
not, then we need to find the disagreement. We move first to
first base — observations. Someone may report that only 5 percent of the employees have used the program. Another may
describe how the program helped an employee overcome a drug
problem. Another may have the data on how much it costs per
employee. We may discover that instead of disagreeing, we simply had different information. Sharing these differences only increases our understanding of the total situation.

If we can agree on the relevant observations for answering our question, then we can move to second base — value judg-

ments. Some may hold that the organization has an obligation to help employees. Others may look at the benefits versus the costs or point out that promoting good health is in line with the organization's overall goals. These different value judgments can also enrich the discussion. Even disagreements can help group members to understand the strengths and weaknesses of their positions. As the members begin to question each other's values, they naturally move on to third base — assumptions. Here some may argue that people only become strong if they are left alone, while others may believe that we all belong to the same family. If we can agree on the assumptions that impinge on the issue, then we can go for home plate.

Working around the bases may have changed our minds or may have generated other policy proposals. Differences at any base may stop our run. In either case, going around the diamond has at least uncovered the resources available for decision making. Even if it seems impossible to "get to first base" with some people, knowing the resources for "getting home" can help us make a better decision. Since it is easy to confuse these resources because we usually use them jointly, we need to identify them and then move on to develop criteria for evaluating them.

Policy Proposals. Proposals about what we should do are answers to questions. Sometimes we forget this fact and treat proposals as isolated statements or, even worse, as answers to questions other than the one that the speaker has in mind. Does the proposal to cut employee assistance programs answer a question about how to balance the budget or a question about the appropriate benefits for employees? If it is the first question, we will want to look at a variety of ways to balance the budget. If it is the second, we will want to consider the entire benefit package. To agree or disagree with a policy, we need to know what question it answers. Also, by consciously beginning our ethical reflections with questions about what should be done, we ensure that everyone is working on the same question. Even when we move into discussions about value judgments and assumptions, we can direct these discussions by keeping the central question in focus.

To evaluate proposals, we need to examine the reasons that support them. We need to ask a simple and yet fundamental question in ethical reflection—the question "Why?" If you ask why someone believes we should adopt a certain policy, she or he will inevitably point to observations, value judgments, or assumptions that support the conclusion. By examining these supports, we can discover the grounds on which the proposal is based and we can then better assess its strengths and weaknesses. Roger Fisher and William Ury make a similar point in their *Getting to Yes* when they say that you should begin negotiation not on the positions people take but on the interests— observations and value judgments—that lead people to take them (1987, pp. 41f.). To investigate different policy proposals, we need to shift from a stance of judging which policy has the most merit to a stance of inquiring into a policy's background. A stance of inquiry not only allows the group to entertain opposing views but also saves the conversation from becoming trapped in either-or dilemmas. Moral language too easily takes us into such dilemmas, because it tends to frame proposals as either right or wrong. In many organizational settings, however, we may find more than two alternatives. To uncover them, we need to focus on the original question and see what other proposals we can develop rather than defending only our own proposals. As the whole group mutually inquires into different proposals, it can discover what support the different positions can actually muster.

People's Observations. How we answer the question about what we should do depends a lot on changes in our environment and in our responses to these changes. Managers may argue for increased child-care facilities, for example, because more employees need them, or for more corporate involvement in the community because of the community's increased needs. Our descriptions of changes, of course, are never totally objective. We always interpret situations from a particular perspective and for a reason. In most cases, however, we can distinguish between a descriptive statement of what happened and an evaluative statement of what it means. If I say I am overloaded with work, I have made an evaluative statement. If I say I have to finish two reports before the weekend, that is descriptive. People may disagree with the evaluative statement and yet agree with the descriptive one.

The key characteristic of descriptive statements or observations is that they can be verified. "Treating workers with respect increases morale," for example, is an observation because it can be checked out. We can compare different workplaces and see if there is a high correlation between treatment of workers and morale. If I say that we *should* treat workers with respect, however, we cannot investigate whether or not that is true, because it depends on our value judgments. Some statements seem to fall between observations and value judgments. When we hear that people want to be treated with respect, we can take that statement as a generalization from observations or as a belief. You can always ask for evidence to ensure that statements are descriptive and the evidence can resolve most disagreements. Disagreements about observations usually occur because people have different information or give different weight to the information they share. Such disagreements are the easiest to resolve. You do more research if you do not have enough information, or you test it more if it is not yet reliable.

Sometimes you cannot obtain enough information to change anyone's position or the information is impossible to verify, and so the disagreement remains. In many cases, however, people can agree on an action or policy that provides the better course of action in light of what they do know. We seldom have all the facts, so we make the best decision we can with the information we have. We usually make a decision based on enough but not all of the information. If a group cannot come to an agreement after it has reviewed the information and tested its accuracy, the disagreement probably has its source in different values or different assumptions.

Value Judgments. During the Vietnam War, President Johnson chastised his opponents for opposing American policy when they had "inadequate" information for doing so. If they knew what he knew — confidential, of course — then they would support the

American effort. John Bennett, then president of Union Theo-
logical Seminary, responded by saying that the basic disagreement was not over the information but over its interpretation.
In other words, the disagreement resided more on the level of
different beliefs and values than on the level of observations.

Our values determine the worth of things. Our values even
influence the selection and formulation of the facts. There are
no totally value-free observations. When we begin to examine
our values, we also increase our ability to review the depth of
our observations. At the same time, we can make a distinction
between an informational question about what happened and
a value question about what it means. People often agree on
the facts and still disagree about the facts' meaning, because people use different values to evaluate them.

Organizational life is permeated with values. In developing a wage scale, for example, we need to know both the worth
of the various aspects of different jobs and the criteria for setting wages. To accomplish the first task, we may differentiate
jobs based on degree of responsibility, skill level, educational
level, opportunities for training, and so on. These factors constitute some of the organization's values. They also determine
what facts people look for and what they overlook.

While different factors allow us to compare and contrast
different jobs, they do not establish the worth of work. Some
may believe that wages should be paid based on internal equity.
Others may say that wages should be set according to the market. In either case, the criterion becomes a norm for determining what to do — a value judgment. The category of value judgments can refer to a variety of norms we use in making decisions,
including values such as integrity and wealth, ethical principles
or moral standards such as the greatest good for the greatest
number, and the different forms of justice. We will consider these
different kinds of value judgments in Chapters Five and Eight.
Whatever our value judgments, when we begin to investigate
how we use them, we enter the fourth resource for making
decisions — our assumptions.

Assumptions. Our assumptions are those beliefs that we take
for granted. In a sense, they are what we have faith in — what

we count on. We usually become aware of our basic assumptions only when something contradicts them. In the past, many employees assumed that good performance meant continued employment. Recent plant closures and mergers have led many to think they were naive. They *were* naive, but only in the sense that basic assumptions are usually naive, because nothing has caused us to question or analyze them, even though they greatly influence our decisions.

Disagreement about our assumptions may be the most difficult to resolve, because it signals different orientations toward the self, others, and the world. Our assumptions arise out of personal experiences, education, and reflections. Although we make many assumptions, not all are equally relevant to any particular ethical issue. By leaving the investigation of assumptions until the end of the process of ethical reflection, the work we do with observations and value judgments will help us to realize which assumptions need examination. Sometimes, of course, we will not have to look at assumptions, especially if our reflection on observations and value judgments so clarifies the issues that we agree about what to do.

Opposing Views. Groups engage in ethical reflection usually because they do not agree about what should be done. In many cases, the discussion begins with members offering different proposals and giving different reasons to support them. At first, we may interpret an opposing view as hostile and competitive. This competitive stance, however, keeps the group judging rather than investigating. It also prevents the group from utilizing the resources that opposing views offer. Instead of setting up a framework where different views fight against each other, the process of ethical reflection needs a framework where different views increase the available resources for decision making. Instead of assuming a limited number of good ideas, that compete for acceptance, we need to assume an abundance of ideas — maybe even more than we want — where everyone gains by increasing the available resources.

Agreement, of course, is never guaranteed in ethical reflection, but finding out why people disagree can surely help us develop a better course of action. In fact, disagreement is almost

essential for ethical reflection. For most of us, our opinions remain good enough until someone disagrees with us. So we develop a solution that was good enough for a particular problem,
but then instead of leaving the solution there, we carry it on
to other problems; even though a new problem may differ substantially from the original problem, we apply the same good-
enough solution again. To prevent this, most individuals, and
all organizations, need questioners, critical partners, to help test
if our solution is still good enough or if a better alternative exists. An opposing view — the loyal opposition — gives us occasions to find innovative solutions to contemporary problems.

Awareness of these five different kinds of resources not
only increases the possibility of discovering the best decision;
it also prevents many forms of confusing and dysfunctional communication caused by participants speaking to each other about
different resources. While some make observations, others may
evaluate them or even state a policy. An employee may be trying to describe problems in a work situation, for example, while
his or her supervisor speaks about what the organization wants
to accomplish. By focusing on policy rather than attending to
the employee's observations, the supervisor prevents understanding on both sides. If both parties attend to one task at a time,
they can actually stop talking past one another and start talking with one another.

Good listening requires that we clarify what resources a
speaker is using. Sometimes it is important to say, "Wait a
minute. Let's first see if we're both talking about the same thing.
Are we dealing with observations, value judgments, or assumptions?" In everyday talk, of course, we switch back and forth
between different resources and some utterances express more
than one. Through conscious listening, however, we can begin
to discern the type of resource that leads the conversation. As
a way of clarifying the four resources that opposing views can
use, let us look at two different statements, for each resource,
in a discussion about a co-worker with AIDS.

Proposals: *A:*   We should protect people
                           from discrimination.

	B:	AIDS carriers should not be at work.
Observations:	*A:*	AIDS isn't transmitted by casual contact.
	B:	Accidents can happen, and they have.
Value judgments:	*A:*	Individuals have a right to equal treatment.
	B:	The company has an obligation to provide a safe workplace.
Assumptions:	*A:*	We can trust people most of the time.
	B:	The world is a dangerous place.

With these statements, the disagreement between speaker A and speaker B seems pervasive, but at least we can see different avenues of approach to the issue. By reviewing the statements at each of the four resources, perhaps we can locate what topics a discussion should cover and in what order we should address the different disagreements. If the resistance resides on the level of assumptions, for example, then working only on the level of observations will have little effect. Instead, we need to clarify different assumptions and see how appropriate they are to the actual situation. In working on each of the four levels, we need criteria to examine their appropriateness and adequacy.

Criteria for Evaluating the Resources

How can we assess the adequacy or significance of statements about policy proposals, observations, value judgments, or assumptions? What are the appropriate questions to ask? Part of the answer comes from recognizing the level of discourse that belongs to each resource. We express policy proposals in prescriptive terms: "We should do *X*." Our observations are descriptive statements about situations and events. Although our value judgments may appear as descriptive statements ("Everyone has the right to privacy"), they are actually normative, saying how things should be. They are not grounded in our observations but in our assumptions. The difference between descriptive and normative statements parallels the difference between "is" and "ought." The "is" or descriptive level of discourse belongs to the category of observations. The "ought" or normative level belongs to values and beliefs.

Our assumptions, which express our basic understandings of reality, usually take an expository style. Many of our basic assumptions, of course, are rarely spoken, and only if we become attentive to them do they come to light. In most cases, assumptions are what we take for granted. When we do investigate assumptions, we find that they expose how we see things and how we relate to what we see. The appropriate language style for assumptions, therefore, is expressive or expository. The four resources then give us the following levels of discourse:

Resource	*Level of discourse*
Proposals	Prescriptive
Observations	Descriptive
Value judgments	Normative
Assumptions	Expressive

Later in this chapter, when we examine the logic of arguments, we will see how an argument includes and connects prescriptive, descriptive, normative, and expressive statements. Before making these connections, we need to explain the appropriate criteria to use when deciding whether to accept a speaker's statements on any of these levels of discourse. First of all, we need to recognize that not all levels have the same criteria. We experience this all the time. If someone tells me that increasing wages will increase productivity, I can ask for evidence to prove the assertion. Are there instances where increased wages have had that effect? Are there instances where wages have stayed the same and other changes increased productivity? By asking for evidence, I use the criterion of true or false. If someone tells me that we should respect each other, I cannot verify this statement in the same way. It does not refer to observations but to values or ethical principles. I need a different criterion to decide whether to accept the statement. Each of the four resources has its own criterion.

For a policy proposal, the criterion is right or wrong. We want to know if the policy is the right thing to do. Although the policy tells us what to do, if we ask why we should do it, we must turn to the other resources for an answer. Throughout the argumentative process, we search for the right policy, but only after we have examined the facts, value judgments, and assumptions can we determine what it is. So, the policy criterion is right or wrong, but we can only discover and meet the standards of this criterion by investigating the other elements of the argumentative process.

When we assess observations (descriptive statements) instead of using the criterion of right or wrong, we want to know if the description is true or false. We also want to know if it excludes relevant aspects of the situation, so that we do not commit the fallacy of half-truths. We commit this fallacy when we find information to support our position but ignore all the other facts that speak against it. Descriptions that leave out all contrary or opposing data or counterexamples seldom meet the test of inclusiveness — an important standard for making good decisions. Our primary concern is whether the observations truly describe what happened. Whether they do or not can be determined by asking other witnesses, doing our own research, or trying to recreate situations so that we can see for ourselves. For many organizational issues, an effective means of meeting the inclusive test is to make sure that all important constituencies or stakeholders are represented.

Value judgments, however, cannot be understood by simply looking at the facts of the case. Even though facts and values are interdependent, we judge their validity by different standards. When someone states a fact, you can ask if it is true: "Did it really happen?" "Is that how it works?" When we work with facts, we try to verify them. When someone states a value, we do not try to verify it but wonder if we believe the same thing

or hold the same values. We usually agree with someone's belief or value not because it is empirically verifiable but because
it "makes sense" to us. What makes sense agrees somewhat with
our own background and experience and our other beliefs and
values. Therefore, instead of using the criterion of true or false,
for now we use a criterion of humane and practical; we reserve
our full discussion of value judgments for Chapters Five and
Eight.

Our assumptions, too, should be humane and practical,
but these two terms cannot cover all assumptions. Actually, since
our assumptions about ourselves, others, and the world ultimately provide the basis for all other evaluations, they have their
own criteria, such as whether they are consistent, relevant, coherent, and responsive. Perhaps the most effective criterion for
assumptions is responsiveness: "Are the assumptions concerning this situation responsive to its various claims and counter-
claims?" When we match the four resources with their corresponding criteria, we see the following relationships:

Resource	Criterion
Proposals	Right/Wrong
Observations	True/False
Value judgments	Humane/Inhumane
Assumptions	Responsive/Irresponsive

Because the four criteria refer to four aspects of the process
of decision making, we can apply them to any policy statement,
since such statements will implicitly contain these criteria. Let
us see how this works by applying the four criteria to the following statement:

We ought to recruit more female executives.

We can start by applying the proposal criterion by asking if this
is the right thing to do: "Should we recruit more female executives?" Assuming we disagree, we turn to observations. We can
then apply the criterion of true or false by asking about the facts
of the case. Have we made some efforts? Are there women to

be recruited? We can also ask about the value judgments, such as fairness, that this statement implies. Do we have a moral obligation to correct imbalances in the work force? Will this fulfill our obligations to our stakeholders? What are those obligations? Finally, we can ask about what this statement really expresses — what is it responding to? Is this a response to women's experience of being shut out of the higher levels of the work force? Or a public relations ploy? Or both? Or is the talk about bringing more women into executive positions an effort to head off questions about the company's financial performance? Are we aware of the impact this policy will have on men and women in the company? As you see, working with these criteria can generate a multitude of questions, but in the process of ethical reflection, we need to ask only those questions that will further our exploration of the agreements and disagreements among people in the decision-making process. Our purpose is not to ask every possible question but rather to use the different criteria to find the right questions to ask, so we can then discover what we should do. In the actual practice of ethical reflection, the resources and corresponding criteria are combined to develop arguments. We take positions, give reasons to support them, investigate the strengths and weaknesses of opposing views, and try to persuade the group to consent to our proposal. Let us now look at this process.

Coordinating Resources for Decision Making

In our everyday unreflective thinking, we seldom need to make a distinction between thinking about things and thinking about relations, but when we begin to actually put our resources together for making decisions, we do need to make a switch from one to the other. Suppose someone observes a decline in the interaction among co-workers and decides to initiate more joint projects. This seems like a good idea. But when people start to question it, they may think not only about the observation (Is it true?) and the policy (Is it right?) but also about what kind of relationship exists between the observation and the policy. How does one move from the observation to the policy? We can answer such questions once we have understood the logic of ethical reflection.

The Logic of Ethical Reflection

Although a complete analysis of decision making includes all five resources, let us begin with the three usually used in the initial stages of ethical reflection—policy proposals, observations, and value judgments. As stated previously, disagreement usually begins at the level of policy or action. When we are asked why we support a proposal, we answer by referring either to what is happening or to specific value judgments. The relationship of observations and value judgments to policy parallels the relationship of the minor and major premises to the conclusion in the traditional syllogism:

Major premise   Value judgment
Minor premise   Observations
Conclusion   Policy

Just as in the syllogism, where the major premise functions to link the minor premise and the conclusion, so also do our value judgments connect observations and policy. Here is an example:

All employees who increase sales over 20 percent deserve promotions.
Jane increased her sales by 25 percent.
Jane should be promoted.

Our discussion starts again with the "conclusion": "Jane should be promoted." Our supervisor asks why. ("Why?" is one essential tool for ethical analysis.) We answer with relevant information: "She has increased sales by 25 percent." The supervisor does not understand. She asks, "So what?" ("So what?" is another essential tool.) "Oh," we respond, "we believe that anyone who increases sales over 20 percent should be promoted." But then the supervisor replies, "I didn't know that, but I see that if I accept your premise, I have to agree with you."

If the supervisor does not accept the major premise — our value judgment — she will not agree with the conclusion, even when she agrees with the fact that Jane did increase her sales 25 percent. The supervisor will not agree if she does not share the value judgment that serves as a transition between the observation and the policy. The value judgments, in other words, connect the observations and the policy.

The interrelationship between three of the levels of discourse — descriptive, prescriptive, and normative — is shown in Figure 2.

Figure 2.

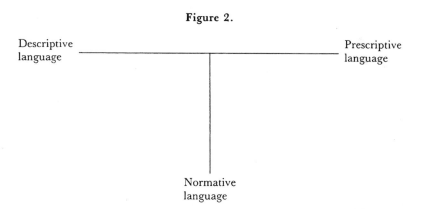

Descriptive
language

Prescriptive
language

Normative
language

Figure 2 depicts the composite nature of ethical reflection. Instead of focusing on only one type of language such as normative or prescriptive, it includes descriptive, prescriptive, and normative. Each is essential and yet each differs from the others. Empirical truths cannot tell you what is prescriptively right: You cannot derive "ought" from "is." While descriptive language shows us what happened, prescriptive language says what should happen, and it needs a justification. We justify by showing the connection — the normative statement — between the description and the prescription.

Suppose that we learn that a majority of employees favor child-care facilities at work. Even if we accept the data as accurate, we still will not know what should be done until we draw inferences from them. People who believe that the workplace should only provide jobs will not find the observation compelling.

People who believe the company should be responsive to the family needs of employees will probably consider developing such centers.

In spite of the emphasis on research in organizational studies, facts do not speak by themselves. They are mute. As perennial interpreters, however, we always give a voice to facts, and so any entity that becomes a fact for us already has meaning from us. What it means depends on our values and beliefs.

We can overlook the essential function of values and beliefs in drawing inferences from observations as long as we work with others who share our values and beliefs. Only disagreement or careful analysis exposes our silent migrations from facts to policy. In many cases, values and beliefs remain unspoken and function as implied premises. Consider the following statements:

1. The directors must like our project, because they continue to fund it.
2. We must have a communication problem, because you never agree with me.
3. Since the company pays the tuition, I should enroll in the program.

Each of these makes sense, but only if we supply the missing premise.

1. The directors must like what they fund.
2. Disagreement means lack of understanding.
3. You should take advantage of every opportunity.

Without the unspoken premises, of course, the statements are incomplete. They lack any connection between the observations and the conclusions. Much of the work of ethical reflection involves determining the implied value judgments of our arguments.

Even though values are necessary for ethical reflection, they are not sufficient. To choose the right policy, we need to know the facts and to work through the possible connections between the facts and various policy options. Furthermore, we need to consider assumptions and opposing views. To include them in the logic of ethical reflection and to understand their function in the development of ethical arguments, we need to expand our triadic model into a more comprehensive argumentative model.

Argumentative Model

The philosopher Stephen Toulmin, in his *The Uses of Argument* (1957) and later in *An Introduction to Reasoning* (Toulmin and others, 1984), has provided a model for arguments that we can convert into a model for relating all five resources (Toulmin, 1957, p. 94). His model (shown in Figure 3) includes five terms: conclusion, data, warrant, backing, and qualification.

Figure 3.

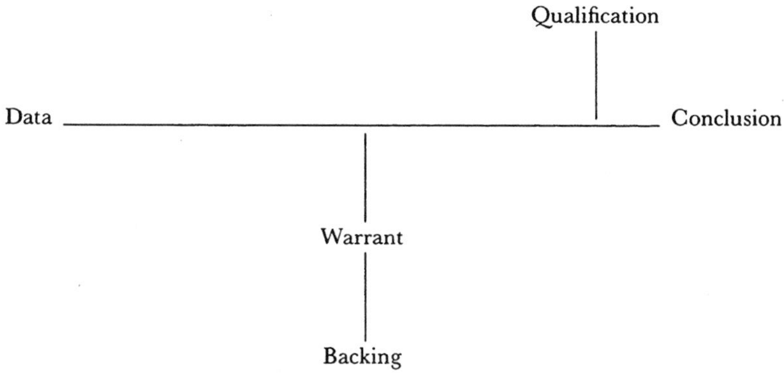

Source: Adapted from Toulmin, 1957, p. 101.

In this model, the three primary terms — *conclusion, data,* and *warrant* — function as the conclusion and two premises in the syllogism. We start with the conclusion, support it with data (or observations), and then supply the warrant for relating the data and the conclusion. The warrant authorizes the move from the data to the conclusion, just as the major premise authorizes the move from the minor premise to the conclusion in the syllogism.

The two terms *backing* and *qualification* come into play either when the warrant needs more support or when there are certain limits or boundaries that may qualify one's conclusion. Toulmin's argumentative model can then be rewritten with the terms of ethical reflection as shown in Figure 4.

Figure 4.

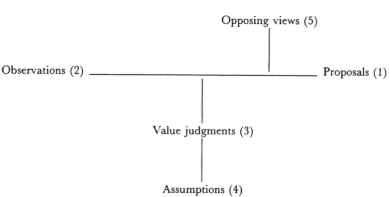

In a typical discussion about a policy proposal, we would start with a proposed policy: "Let us do *X*." Then someone asks, "Why do you think we should?" To answer this question, we move to the observation or information: "Because of the following facts." And then our questioner asks about the connection between the policy and the observation: "But how did you get from these facts to this policy?" Or the person could ask, "What warrants your move between these observations and this policy?" The warrant is a value judgment. Like a major premise, it serves as a transition between the observation and the policy.

The two remaining elements of the revised model — assumptions and opposing views — extend the argument beyond the traditional syllogism. The assumptions give support to the value judgments. Acknowledging the strengths of opposing views allows the speaker to consider the limits of his or her proposal. The model elicits a dialogue that goes something like this:

> "We want to do *X*."
> "Why?"
> "Because of these observations."

"So what?" (How do you connect the observations and
the policy?)
"Because we value *Y.*"
"Why do you value *Y?*"
"Because we assume *Z.*"
"Oh, and what about the opposing views?"
"We want to do *X* unless it destroys their strengths."

Graphically, the process looks like Figure 5, beginning
with number 1 and moving to 5.

Figure 5.

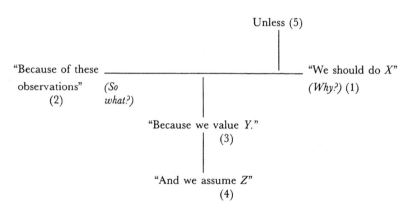

To see how this argumentative model works, we will examine two sides of the issue of whether a corporation's constituencies should have a voice in its management. In some European countries, workers sit on corporate boards of directors,
and there has been some discussion of that in the United States.
In 1990, two large pension fund directors asked for a voice in
General Motors's selection of a new president. Environmental
and other public interest groups as well as civic leaders have
raised such issues, too, and are now on some corporate boards.
Because both sides in this debate have some good reasons for
their positions, it will serve as a useful example for ethical reflection. We can develop arguments for and against the question
of whether corporate constituencies should have a voice in corporate policy.

Should Corporate Constituencies Have a Voice in Corporate Policy?

First, we must ensure that we understand the question we want to answer: "Should the primary constituencies of a corporation — investors, workers, the larger community — have a voice in corporate management decisions?" But what do we mean by "a voice"? Let us say that they have representation without the right to vote at strategic planning and evaluating meetings. Definitions could sidetrack us, but they do not need to, if we remember that the purpose here is to illustrate the argumentative model, not to settle the debate. We need first to develop two proposals, which we will call the constituency proposal (CP) and the management proposal (MP). In their opening statements, CP advocates constituency representation and MP disagrees. We ask them why they have given their answers to our policy question. CP advocates answer, "We think that constituencies should have a voice, because corporate policy affects our well-being." Is this true? It does seem likely. So the observation passes the first test. We ask, "So what?" CP advocates then need to make a connection between the observation and the policy. They need to provide a value judgment. Perhaps they would argue that they should have a say in whatever affects their well-being. This value judgment constitutes a popular norm. If something affects us, then we should have some voice in how it is managed. So CP advocates can diagram their argument as shown in Figure 6.

Figure 6.

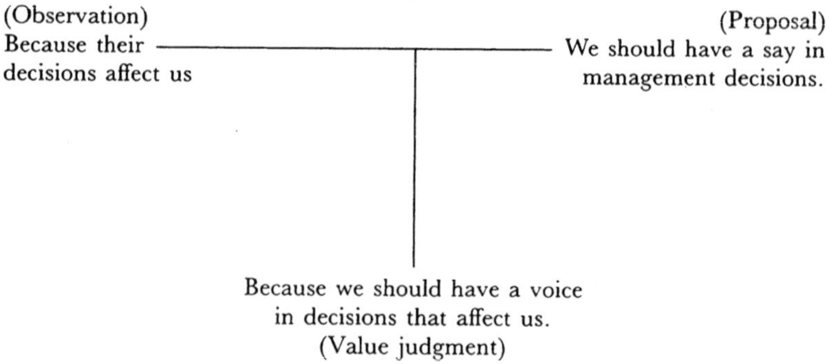

(Observation)   (Proposal)
Because their ——————————————————— We should have a say in
decisions affect us   management decisions.

Because we should have a voice
in decisions that affect us.
(Value judgment)

We can question this value judgment. After all, even the weather affects our well-being, but we do not have much say about that. CP advocates might counter that they mean events that result from selecting one of several options and that the different options will have different effects on them. In other words, they are concerned about decisions made by organizations as moral agents. That seems to clarify the application of the value judgment, and if corporate management does have several options, then the value judgment would seem to connect the observation and the policy. This seems like a good argument, so let us see what we can develop on the other side.

The MP advocates could argue against constituency representation on corporate boards because these representatives would be, as they say, "outsiders." Let us take the term *outsiders* as meaning those who do not share the interests of the corporation and do not really know the ins and outs of corporate life — how things really work. We then need to evaluate this description as an observation: "Is it true?" We could do some investigation to find out. For example, we could give a set of prospective representatives a kind of test to see if they know much about corporate life or if they at least recognize corporate interests. Let us assume, for the sake of the argument, that they took such a test, perhaps through interviews, and we discovered that the observation was true. They were outsiders as we have defined the term. To continue the argument, we need to find the link between this observation and the policy. We can ask, "So they are outsiders. So what?" MP advocates need to develop a value judgment such as "corporations should be directed by insiders." Insiders, let us say, means those who "belong" to the corporation and share the corporate interests. Here we need to remember the distinction between "is" and "ought." The value judgment does not say that corporations are directed by persons who belong but rather that they should be. The argument then looks like Figure 7.

We have said that we agree with the observation, but do we agree with the value judgment? Perhaps we need to investigate it further. What else could the term *insiders* refer to? Or what assumption could we supply that would make it stronger? Remember, in developing these arguments, we want to find the

Figure 7.

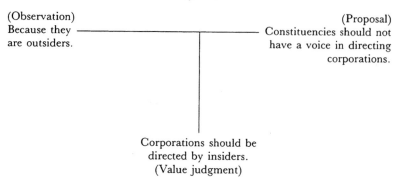

(Observation)
Because they
are outsiders.

(Proposal)
Constituencies should not
have a voice in directing
corporations.

Corporations should be
directed by insiders.
(Value judgment)

strengths of all sides, not their weaknesses. It is the strengths that become the best resources for making the right decision. What comes to mind is the question "How do you get inside?" Perhaps you get inside by being chosen. If so, then MP advocates may assume that the corporation has a right to choose its board members. This gives us an assumption that helps us to understand the MP advocates' argument. Americans, of course, place a high priority on freedom and free choice, and so the argument seems fairly strong. How strong, and what other rights could be included here? Let us answer that question in Chapter Eight, which examines rights and justice.

When we look at the two arguments, we find that it is fairly easy to verify the observations. If corporate decisions do affect the well-being of the various constituencies, the evidence should be available. If constituent representatives do not understand corporate life or share corporate interests, we can find that out, too. But should they share corporate interests? That question is a value judgment that may affect the significance of constituents' status as outsiders. Actually, their interest in being on the board is to represent interests that differ from corporate interests or at least differ from the ways in which some corporations define their interests. The question of corporate interests and constituency interests, in fact, is probably one of the most fruitful places to continue the discussion. To understand these relations adequately, we need to bring in a systems analysis of the corporation and its constituencies. This analysis not only will help us see the character of the interdependent relationships but also will allow us to address the issue of corporate and constituency power. Chapters Seven and Eight will explore these issues. Even if we do discover a strong link between corporate and constituency interest, however, we have only developed agreement on the level of observations, still leaving the disagreement on the level of value judgments.

We need to find some connection between the CP advocates' value judgment that they should have a say about decisions that affect them and the MP advocates' value judgment that the corporation should choose who should get "inside" and who should participate in their decision-making process. Is there some way we can bring the strengths of each value judgment together? We can try by developing more questions or hypotheses that include both value judgments. For example, we can ask about the MP advocates' value judgment, "Should corporations make decisions that seriously harm their constituencies when input from these constituencies would have persuaded them to select a different course of action?" On the one hand, you could argue that corporations have the right to make a mistake — that is, to make a decision that they later discover was wrong. On the other hand, if a corporation could have prevented the mistake by giving constituencies a voice, then do they not have an obligation to do so?

We can also address the CP advocates' value judgment: "Should constituencies be allowed to influence corporate decisions when they have primarily their own interests in mind and not the interests of the corporation?" This question brings up the question of possible mutual interests again, but it can also help lead us to a discussion of the character of corporate or organizational life, perhaps exposing more assumptions that will eventually bring us to a set of common values that can assign responsibility in an equable manner. However, we have accomplished quite a bit so far. At least, by moving through the argumentative process, we have seen some of the places of disagreement as well as places to work on the development of agreements. We have also seen some strategies of dealing with disagreements, which the next chapter addresses more fully.

Ethical Reflection as Argumentative Analysis

I have argued in this chapter that engaging in ethical reflection can enable organizations to develop better policies. This development becomes possible because the process of reflection increases the resources for decision making. Our implied premise is that increasing one's resources will increase the quality of one's decisions. Behind this premise resides another, of course, which holds that people will tend to use resources appropriately, which finally depends on our assumption that persons are moral agents — persons who possess the power and freedom to choose the right course of action.

The process outlined here is a kind of "argumentative analysis." For some, arguing and analyzing may seem poles apart. Some people may believe that people who argue all the time never really examine their premises or take seriously their opponents' views. Analysts, on the other hand, never enter the public arena with any of the passion of the truly argumentative person. Instead of either of these views, argumentative analysis uses differences to expand and understand the various resources for decision making, coordinates them, and then utilizes their strengths to make the right decision. You can practice such an argumentative analysis by using the worksheet for ethical reflections, the worksheet for developing arguments, and the argumentative map found in Chapter Eleven.

Chapter Four

Forging Agreements from Disagreements and Opposing Views

Individuals, groups, and organizations can have very different attitudes about disagreement. Some seem to assume a world of scarcity where one person's gain is another's loss. In such a world, disagreement usually threatens individuals and blocks communication. What can be interpreted as "other," they interpret as "enemy." Anyone else's gain is seen as their loss. This win-lose mentality usually prevents inquiry into the merits of opposing or different proposals about what should be done. A closely related attitude that also limits our ability to deal with disagreement assumes that people are called on only to say what they know but never to ask about what they do not know. Successful ethical reflection requires that participants both provide and elicit material for discussion. When groups can become open to considering different views, they discover more than they knew before. This "more than we knew before" is the promise of ethical reflection. Ethical reflection can increase an organization's resources by having each party consider different ideas about what should be done instead of defensively maintaining its position and closing the door to other information. To slightly rephrase an old cliche: Disagreement is the mother of invention and innovation.

Disagreement not only promotes the discovery of new ideas but also nurtures agreement. The logic of disagreement runs like this: To disagree with others in organizations requires a degree of trust. Trust requires a mutual commitment to something (such as the organization's purpose), and mutual commitment generates agreement. As we discover the sources of disagreement, we will also uncover even deeper sources of agreement.

In fact, disagreement requires agreement. Only when we agree on some things, on at least one element in the decision-making process, can we disagree on others. If we do not find this agreement, then the disagreement will end in exposing the alienation that actually exists within the organization or between an organization and the larger community. We always take this risk in arguing. Since the fundamental agreements are difficult to know beforehand, however, we usually find them only through the process of ethical reflection.

Acknowledging opposing views as a potential resource has other consequences for ethical reflections. It moves us out of an either-or dilemma, a dilemma that ethics itself sometimes unfortunately creates. If we formulate issues as having only one right answer, then every answer is either right or wrong. In many cases, however, if we permit all parties to participate we have more than two alternatives. Instead of approaching the discussion with a stance of "if I am right, you must be wrong," we can look for possibilities of several alternative contributions in the search for the best answer: "Let us see what support we can develop for our different positions." By agreeing on a ground rule that everyone's argument will receive not only a careful listening but also questions and analysis, we can begin to establish the type of group climate that will encourage exploration into different arguments.

Naturally, we believe that our position is right, but that does not necessarily mean that the other position is wrong. As we saw in the discussion of whether corporate constituencies should have a voice in management policy, both sides can develop strong arguments with which many people will probably agree. This is not unusual. You can understand this by considering the following statement:

> People usually do what they think is right
> considering the world in which they think they live.

Do you agree? I find that many people do. Perhaps this statement says too much. After all, people do commit wrong acts. The statement suggests, however, that people want to justify what they do. Few people actually decide that a certain act is wrong and then choose to do it. Rather, they try as hard as possible to construe their world so that they can justify what they do. Therefore, to understand different positions, we need to understand how those who advocate those positions interpret the world — that is, we need to ask about the observations, value judgments, and assumptions that make up their worldview.

Ethical Standards and Policy Differences

Considering different observations, value judgments, and assumptions may seem contrary to a common view of ethics as taking a stand on what is right and wrong. Whether our view differs from this common view of ethics depends on where we take a stand in the process of ethical reflection. To automatically take a stand on policy or a particular act would certainly limit one's flexibility, and yet that is sometimes seen as the only thing to do. If you consider the different elements of the argumentative process — policy proposals, observations, value judgments, and assumptions — you see that we really have four places to take a stand. Let us investigate each one. Taking a stand on one's observations seems a bit odd, since observations can be verified by empirical evidence. Why not let the evidence demonstrate whether your observations or generalizations have merit? Taking a stand on assumptions does make sense, since that is what we really stand on. Our basic assumptions — especially those we may not even consciously recognize — provide us with our basic orientation for taking a stand at any other place. At the same time, taking a stand on assumptions when we have not examined them seems questionable. We could take a stand on our value judgments, which also makes sense. In fact, do our value judgments not provide the basis for taking any ethical stand at all? It is our commitment to such value judgments as justice and human dignity or doing good and not causing harm that makes up our moral character. So we can certainly take a stand there. We can also take a stand on what should be done (policy), but when the stand here is absolute, it blocks off participation in the complete process of ethical reflection. Furthermore, it ignores the distinctions between value judgments and action proposals and between normative and prescriptive statements.

Dissolving the difference between value judgment and action or policy—collapsing them into one factor—leaves little place for the discussion of observations. Because value judgments have been moved into the policy location, they no longer function as a bridge between observation and policy. In such cases, new observations that actually speak against the policy will have less chance of a hearing. Collapsing value judgments and policy into one also forces us to become inflexible at the level of policy. It assumes we can affirm a value judgment in only one way, which may not be true.

For example, in the drug-testing debate, proponents of drug testing could take a stand either for a particular drug-testing policy or on a value judgment such as worker safety that may support it. Whether worker safety does support the argument for drug testing depends on the evidence of drug abuse, its affect on the work environment, and so forth. If proponents take a stand on the policy, however, they may prevent themselves from discovering such evidence that could either strengthen or weaken their position. They also lose the possibility of finding other and perhaps more effective ways of affirming their concern for worker safety. Taking a stand on worker safety, in contrast, allows managers to evaluate a particular drug-testing policy in terms of an organization's climate and community, and perhaps to discover other policies that promote worker safety. A Volvo plant in Sweden, for example, moved the responsibility for worker safety from management to the labor union, resulting in a dramatically reduced number of accidents. This was not done in response to drug abuse but suggests that workers may know best how to handle their own safety issues, including the issue of drugs. These possibilities will escape those who take their stand on policy rather than on value judgments.

Taking a stand on policy rather than on values overlooks the distinction between what one should try to achieve and how to achieve it. Especially with complex issues, this distinction has enormous importance. Let us say your organization has decided to pursue a course of action that you consider wrong, and, furthermore, you have some information that does not seem to have received the consideration it deserves. You must decide what to do. Should you share the information? If you decide to, then you face a second decision: With whom and how should you share it? These are strategic decisions that depend on a host of factors. You will only consider these factors, however, if you keep in mind the distinction between your value judgment — what is worthwhile to do — and your policy issues — what you should do. If you take a stand on the value judgment and remain flexible about the policy, then your action may not only be "right" but also may result in some good.

Even the issue of honesty can benefit from this distinction between value judgment and policy. Is honesty the best policy? Yes, but it is also a policy, supported by such value judgments as integrity and respect for others. By keeping policy and value judgment separate, you maintain the freedom to decide how to affirm integrity and respect for others in specific situations. You can decide how you tell the truth, when to tell it, and to whom to tell it. While I certainly affirm the importance of ethical standards, and will analyze some standards in Chapters Five and Eight, I also view standards as one element in the process of ethical reflection. They function as value judgments, not as policies. At times, of course, people will find that one policy proposal fulfills their value judgments better than any others, and they can develop arguments to convince others. Even if others are not convinced, these people may still advocate their chosen policy, but by grounding their choice in value judgments, they will remain open to new information and changing circumstances. Ethics certainly considers standards, but when these become only standards of behavior — what people should do — rather than standards for making decisions, then ethics will not have much to contribute to addressing the complex issues of complex organizations. The distinction between value judgment and policy should allow persons to honor their values and to consider different policy proposals or, in other words, to consider differences and deal with disagreements.

Strategies for Dealing with Differences

After eliciting as many serious policy proposals as a group can develop, we need to switch to investigating the observations, value judgments, and assumptions that support them. People with opposing views may have other information or even different interpretations of the data. Sharing the information will increase the whole group's understanding of what is going on. Other people may also use different value judgments, and, by knowing these value judgments, we can see whether these values should be part of any final decision. For example, we may argue against testing workers for drugs at work because such testing invades workers' privacy. Our opponents may argue for drug testing because it can help create a safe workplace. Many of us agree with both of these value judgments — the right to privacy and the need for a safe workplace. So, although we disagree about what should be done, we agree on two important values. This agreement can assist both parties in working together to develop a more comprehensive proposal that incorporates both values — that is, a policy that protects privacy and provides a safe workplace.

The disagreement can also reside on the level of assumptions. In the case of drug testing, some may assume that whatever management does is for the sake of controlling the workplace, while others may assume that management has a genuine concern for worker and product safety. If the disagreement resides here and can be brought into discussion, then people have a chance to examine their basic attitudes toward each other. When people disagree, sometimes we can use the disagreement to develop a new policy proposal, to set the limits of our own proposal, and to monitor policy implementation. Let us start with the last one.

Using Disagreement to Monitor Policy Implementation. Sometimes, after examining the facts, values, and assumptions of different parties, each party may believe that its policy is still the right one. At a staff meeting of a medium-sized consulting company, discussed in Chapter One, people argued for several hours about whether or not to work for a client that manufactured the fuel for nuclear weapons. Some thought their company should not facilitate the productivity of the nuclear weapon industry, while others thought they should. The staff shared their different values and assumptions about their mission, the client organization, and themselves as professionals. The differences were accepted and respected, but no one changed his or her mind. When it came time to decide, the group was split evenly. The executive committee later made the decision that individual consultants could decide for themselves whether to work on the project. One probable result of this discussion, however, was that those who decided to work on it gained a criterion by which to judge their future activities. They could use the opposing view as a kind of "loyal opposition" to monitor the implementation of their decision. In this sense, it increases the resources for the organization and may prevent it from moving further in this direction than it wants to go.

The views of the corporate constituencies, as discussed in Chapter Three, could perform a similar role for the corporate board. The constituencies' claim that corporate decisions affect their well-being could be used to monitor the corporate board's decisions. Using the opposing views as a monitor could help the corporation to correct a policy mistake as it becomes apparent.

Using Disagreement to Qualify Policy. Sometimes it is possible to do more with opposing views than merely to use them for monitoring policy implementation. They can be used to prevent a policy from overextending itself. This is our second strategy for using opposing views.

Some time ago, at a hospital retreat, administrators from the different departments were asked to participate in an unusual experiment: to define the hospital from their perspective assuming that they could realize all their goals for the hospital. Using the current language of organizational management, we labeled the different groups as "driven" by their particular interest. They divided into the following groups:

Group 1: Driven by professional standards
Group 2: Driven by the need for health care
Group 3: Driven by financial performance
Group 4: Driven by social responsibility
Group 5: Driven by technological development
Group 6: Driven by the market

These different groups came up with very different descriptions of the kind of hospital they wanted. The professional standards group described a teaching hospital that allocated resources for research and development, professional training, and "interesting" clients. The second group, driven by the need for health care, represented patients and the public. They envisioned a hospital engaged in care for the sick, involved in the community, and meeting the diverse needs of the population, including preventive needs. The group driven by financial performance wanted a profit-making hospital, with short-term and long-term strategies to expand in an extremely competitive market. The group driven by social responsibility wanted a hospital working with other community agencies helping to solve some of the private and public health problems at home and at work. They were interested in community representation on the hospital board and community input in the decision-making process. The fifth group, driven by technological development, wanted resources invested in modern technology and research facilities. They tended to side with the professional standards group. The final group, driven by the market, wanted more resources allocated to marketing research and advertising, with the goal of securing a market share and a niche for the hospital.

As these groups each developed their own vision of the hospital, pretending that they would be given all they wanted, it became clear that the groups actually needed each other. The hospital needed the proposals of all of the groups, but it could not satisfy any one of them if it meant another would be totally neglected. In other words, each opposing voice represented a healthy limit for the other voices. Without these limits, a single voice would become too loud — a solo voice when a chorus was needed.

The groups began seeing how they could help each other set limits. The hospital wanted to increase professional standards until those increased standards began to hinder the delivery of health care services. The hospital wanted to provide services to those in need but had to consider financial constraints. The hospital needed financial viability, but that viability should not divert the hospital from its social responsibility. The different views, in other words, were necessary for keeping each other in check. This principle, of course, serves as the basis for the governmental division of power among the legislative, executive, and judicial branches in the United States. An old principle, but it has not lost its significance.

In the argumentative model, opposing views that have the function of limiting one's policy fit in the slot for qualifications. There we can use the strengths of opposing views to qualify our own. These qualifications, as the meeting with the hospital administrators demonstrates, actually strengthen one's position rather than diminishing it. Again, our model differs from that of the ethical fanatic who considers any "qualification" of a position to be giving in to the opposition and whose true ethical hero never budges from his position, no matter what the cost. Instead of following this ethical trend, ethical reflection needs to follow the strengths of different positions and to disregard their weaknesses. In the drug-testing controversy, for example, one side argued against drug testing because it violates privacy, and the other side argued for drug testing because it ensures worker safety. Both of these values have merit, and both sides would probably recognize that fact, so each could use the other's value as a qualification of their own view. The first would then say, "We should not engage in drug testing unless we cannot develop any other means of ensuring worker safety." The second could respond by saying, "And we should test for drugs unless we discover that it actually violates the dignity of individuals." Such qualifications can prevent each side from overextending its policy so far that it destroys other value judgments to which it adheres.

Using Disagreement to Develop New Policy Proposals. Sometimes it is possible to move beyond using disagreements either as a monitor for policy implementation or as a policy qualifier and instead to use them for policy formation. This use requires that people change their minds, which is something that cannot be taken for granted but does happen. We usually change our minds because we learn something we did not know before or focus on something we had not given enough attention to. Ethical reflection as a learning process means that participants can move from what they already know to what they did not know before. They may discover good reasons for views they disagree with, and these good reasons may appear as something they would have accepted had they been aware of them. For this change to occur, participants will need an inquiring mind.

Although a learning stance toward organizational issues will encourage change, such a stance by itself will probably not suffice. We need some direction in the process of forging new agreements, which can then generate a policy different than either party had thought of before. We can engage in such a process by taking the following steps: (1) analyze the initial arguments to discover their implied value judgments and assumptions; (2) find the key terms in the value judgments and use them to form a new common value judgment; and (3) transfer any remaining disagreement to the level of observation, where it has a better chance of resolution because we can bring empirical evidence and research to settle any differences.

In Chapter Three, we began this process by looking for connections between the value judgments of corporate autonomy and constituent representation. We then developed questions concerning rights and justice — questions that can only be answered with the aid of a systems approach, which will be developed in Chapter Seven. Let us now narrow our focus to one constituent and analyze arguments for and against workers participating in workplace management. Such a debate can illustrate how to move from unrelated to related value judgments.

Arguing About Participatory Management

Should workers participate in the management of their workplace? Management might argue that since managers are hired to run the business, they should control the work force. Workers, in contrast, might argue that since they are doing the work, they should have a say in what goes on. At this stage of the debate, each group advocates a different policy, supporting it with different arguments.

We can begin our analysis with these two different arguments. The workers appeal to the fact that they do the work.

We can imagine that management may agree with this fact and yet disagree with the workers' policy. "So what?" management can ask. "Just because you do the work does not mean that you should control how it is done." Management's argument, in contrast, appeals to contractual relations. Controlling the work is part of management's job description. After all, managers manage. Can the workers disagree with this? Yes, they can, because they know that what *is* does not tell us what *ought to be*. Workers can also respond, "So what? Just because management has such a job description does not mean that that is how it should be. Maybe we should rewrite your job description." Since the debate concerns what *should* be rather than what *is,* basing one's argument on existing relations does little to resolve the conflict.

At this point, each argument is missing a value judgment that connects observations with policies. Management's observation is the argument that workers should not control their own work because that is the manager's job. We need to discover what value judgment would allow management to move from this observation to their policy proposal. They could say, "We should respect existing contracts," which would fulfill the necessary function of a value judgment for management's argument, but the other side would probably not accept it. Still, we can probe this value judgment and see if we can find behind it a more inclusive belief that both sides will accept. So we start with the following exchange:

> *Worker:*   Why should we respect existing contracts?
>
> *Manager:*   Because that maintains order in the company.
>
> *Worker:*   But if we want to change the order, then we must change the contracts. Instead of respecting contracts, we need to respect the work force.
>
> *Manager:*   OK. But you still need to have institutional roles, assigned responsibilities, and accountability. That is what the ex-

isting contracts establish, and that is important for the productivity of the company.

Following this exchange, we can now diagram management's
argument as shown in Figure 8.

Figure 8.

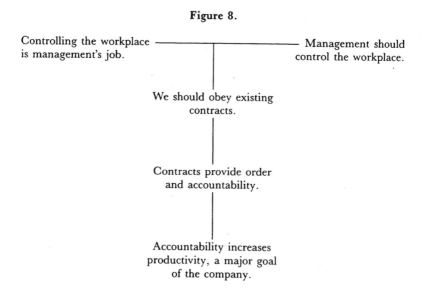

Probing the value judgment has brought us to a belief
that still supports management's policy, but now both sides may
subscribe to it: "Accountability increases productivity." Now let
us turn to the workers' argument and see if we can find a value
judgment that fits it that the managers might accept. The workers argue that they should have control over their work because
they do the work. How can this argument make sense? To discover the value judgments and assumptions implied here, we
can ask, "What would I have to believe to agree with this?" We
might have to believe that people who do the work have important knowledge about what they do and that their work proce-
dure affects the quality of their work, but these statements are
still observations about the workplace. We need a value or be-

lief that connects these observations to the workers' policy proposal. We can say that in terms of job security and promotions, workers are accountable for their work. They too pay the costs of poor productivity. To finish their argument, we need only to assume that people who are accountable for something should also have control over it. So their argument now looks like Figure 9.

Figure 9.

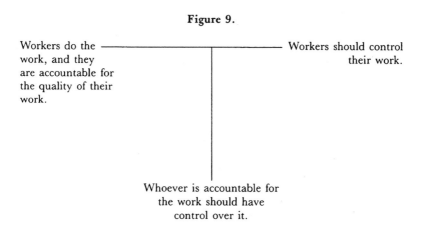

Workers do the work, and they are accountable for the quality of their work. ——————— Workers should control their work.

Whoever is accountable for the work should have control over it.

Let us compare the two value judgments we have developed:

| Accountability increases productivity, a major goal of the company. | Whoever is accountable for the work should control it. |

What are the major terms? *Accountability, productivity,* and *control.* How should these terms be related? We ask that question because we want to take the value judgments of each side and try to develop a statement that each will agree with. Accountability and control certainly belong together. Would you not agree that if someone is held accountable for something he or she should be given control over it? That could be our basic belief that both sides agree with. It serves as the criterion for determining what should be done. So now the arguments for worker control look like Figure 10.

Figure 10.

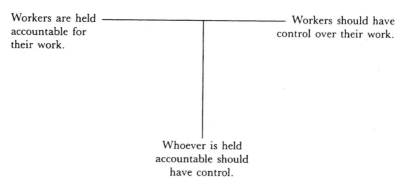

The argument for the management position looks like Figure 11.

Figure 11.

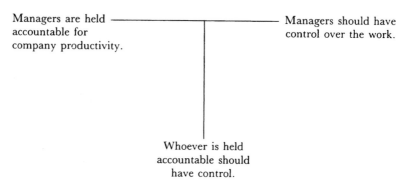

The disagreement now rests at the level of observation. We can investigate the lines of accountability, which will differ in different work settings. The accountability of air-traffic controllers, for example, will differ from the accountability of shop welders. It is different for nurses than for clerks. In most cases, instead of accountability belonging to either employers or workers, it belongs to both. The debate does not end here, but the stage has been set for a more fruitful discussion. To whom and for what are employers and employees accountable? How should we balance accountability, job definition, and productivity?

Let us review what has transpired in this fictional dialogue. It started with two groups asserting conflicting policies and giving reasons. The reasons referred to the existing state of affairs. We then turned to the implied premises or value judgments that would connect these observations (what is) to their policy proposals (what ought to be). After finding the initial beliefs of the groups, we probed them to see if we could find more general beliefs that both sides might accept. We wanted to find a common value or belief that would serve as the criterion for evaluating the observations and for connecting different observations to policy proposals. We were successful because we assumed that both sides would agree to some connection between accountability and control. This principle is really a form of justice or fairness. It states that there should be a reasonable proportion between two different activities — accountability and control. At this point, we can leave the parties to work out the actual distribution of accountability and control for their situations.

The forging of agreements on value judgments will not always be possible. Sometimes value judgments are based on very different assumptions and arise out of very different traditions and cultures. Sometimes we cannot discover a value judgment that is both inclusive and convincing. We can say, for example, that we all value respect for persons or want to achieve the organization's objective, but these values can mean very different things to different people. Effective ethical reflection requires that we have competence in using different value judgments and that we can explain their strengths and weaknesses to other participants. Therefore, the next chapter discusses some value judgments that can serve as guides for evaluating our initial arguments as well as providing us with strategies for developing appropriate questions to analyze specific cases.

Chapter Five

Analyzing the Organization and Its Actions

In the discussion of worker control, we developed a value judgment that allowed both sides to negotiate a policy on the basis of accountability. This kind of value judgment rests on a notion of justice that distributes control according to accountability. As we will see in Chapter Eight, theories of justice play a significant role in organizational responsibility. Other ethical theories can also facilitate ethical reflection by clarifying disagreements and by interpreting or reframing issues so that groups can arrive at a responsible decision. What we need are value judgments that cover the areas where people can disagree. What are these areas? Kenneth Burke suggests the following: "Men may violently disagree about the purposes behind a given act, or about the character of the person who did it, or how he did it, or in what kind of situation he acted, or they may even insist upon totally different words to name the act itself. But be that as it may, any complete statement about motives will offer *some kind of* answer to these five questions: what was done (act), when or where it was done (scene), who did it (agent), how he did it (agency), and why (purpose)" (1969, p. xv). Burke calls these five terms — *act, scene, agent, agency,* and *purpose* — a *pentad* and argues that if we consider human events as activities or actions rather than as movements or behaviors, then these terms will give us a comprehensive framework for analyzing human action. You may have noticed that Burke's terms parallel the traditional journalistic questions of What? When? Where? Who? How? and Why? While answers to these questions can give us information about the different elements of human action, we really need to know about the relationships among the elements. We also need to know which element is primary and what influence the elements have on each other. Does the scene — the situation — determine the act? Does the agent — the actor or the decision-making group — determine the purpose, or does the scene determine the purpose? Some will emphasize the "who" question, which will lead them to consider a person's character or intentions as the decisive element in making value judgments. Others will start with the agent's or organization's purpose. Another group may only consider the act itself and then allow the other four factors to fall where they may around "doing the right thing." Burke's pentad suggests that these different views are incomplete if they fail to consider the other elements of the pentad. We need a set of value judgments that will include all five terms of the pentad, so that disagreements about any one of them can be resolved by looking at their relationships and at the whole picture.

This chapter presents three ethical theories that, taken together, cover all five terms. At the same time, each theory is complete in itself, with its own method for arriving at a right decision. The theories' traditional labels are *teleology, deontology,* and *utilitarianism,* but can be named by their primary criteria for justifying actions: an ethics of purpose, an ethics of principle, and an ethics of consequence. An ethics of purpose uses an agent's goal or vision as its criterion. An ethics of principle evaluates acts according to their implicit rule or principle. An ethics of consequence examines probable results. These three ethics provide three different answers to the question "Why should we choose a specific policy?", as shown below:

Ethics	*Answer*
Purpose	"Because it accomplishes our purpose."
Principle	"Because it can be made into a moral principle."
Consequence	"Because it has positive consequences."

In regard to the five areas of possible disagreement, an ethics of purpose covers agent, purpose, and act. It begins with the agent — either an individual, group, or organization — discovers its purpose, and then uses the purpose to evaluate the act. An ethics of principle focuses on the act and the agent. It determines whether or not the act can conform to a moral rule and then asks why the agent should obey it. An ethics of consequence covers the areas not covered by the other two approaches — agency and the scene or situation. It begins with the act's consequences, by looking at what the act will bring about (agency), and then evaluates it in terms of its effect on the situation (scene). By using all three approaches, we will not only bring into our reflections the possible areas of disagreement but also the means of evaluating their strengths and weaknesses and their relationships with each other.

To use these ethical approaches effectively, we need to know something about them so that we can answer such questions as "How do we know what purposes to choose?" "What acts will achieve our purpose?" "How do we know what moral rule to use in justifying an act, and why should we obey it?" and "What consequences should we consider, and how should we evaluate them?" Actually, the answers to these questions reside in the development of the ethical approaches. They are questions that the approaches were developed to answer. By learning something about the approaches' development, we can also learn how to use them. To ensure that we understand how we can use each approach in actual situations and to see how the approaches complement each other in interpreting a situation, we will use them to analyze the following case.

> Ralph W. was a man in his mid-twenties who had become medically addicted to opiates while undergoing a series of operations and rehabilitative therapy following an accident some years earlier. As a result of the addiction, he is now in a methadone-treatment program and comes regularly to the outpatient clinic at City Hospital. The staff knows that he also gets other drugs outside the hospital, but only pills and tablets of various sorts. On a recent visit to the outpatient clinic, the patient was mistakenly given ten times his usual dose of methadone. He went into cardiac arrest, and was successfully resuscitated. Suspecting a methadone overdose, the physician in charge immediately ordered that an antagonist drug be given to counteract it. After

careful monitoring and continued treatment, Ralph recovered, with no sign of adverse effect from the cardiac arrest. Should Ralph W. be told what caused his cardiac arrest? Should he be informed that he received an overdose of methadone, and that the overdose was the result of a medical error?

The staff claims that the patient's behavior toward them had changed since the episode, and that he now expressed a fear of obtaining drugs on the street. Prior to the cardiac arrest, Ralph had manipulated the staff, had demanded their time and attention, and had seemed unconcerned about the possible dangers of using drugs obtained through nonmedical channels. Since the episode, however, he had become more humble and accepting of the staff's regimen, and was now much less manipulative. Apparently, Ralph believed his own behavior was responsible for bringing on the cardiac arrest, probably from pills he had consumed outside the methadone-treatment program. His belief that he had "done it to himself" seems to have contributed to his improved behavior toward the staff, as well as instilling in him a fear of taking drugs without medical supervision. [From MORTAL CHOICES, by Ruth Macklin, pp. 25–28. Copyright © 1987 by Ruth Macklin. Reprinted by permission of Pantheon Books, a division of Random House, Inc.]

Although this incident happened in an outpatient clinic, it raises questions that many managers face: "What should you do when you have made a mistake?" "Does the result of the case—in this case, Ralph's improved behavior—make any difference?" "How do our decisions in such cases affect the organization's total life?" As we learned from the Watergate affair, the choices we make in dealing with mistakes can even topple a president. Also, the above case allows us to raise questions about an organization's purpose, the quality of human action, and the consequences of our acts—questions that can be transferred to most organizational issues. To evaluate acts from the perspective of an organization's goals, we begin with the ethics of purpose.

Ethics of Purpose

This ethical tradition, with its roots in the writings of Aristotle (384–322 B.C.), provides us with a two-step approach to discovering the right action: first determine the proper end, and then discern the appropriate means for achieving it. The proper purpose or *telos,* which is Greek for "final end," serves as the criterion for justifying the means. In other words, the end justifies the means. Even though this phrase has received much criticism, some of it deserved, many of us still think within a means/end framework: "Getting a degree becomes a means to the end of gaining credentials for a promotion." "Putting in overtime is a means for finishing the project." "Developing an organization's mission statement (its 'ends') serves as a guide for directing the company (the 'means')." But how do we know if we have selected the correct end or purpose?

This was not much of a problem for Aristotle, because his worldview was purposeful. He begins his *Nicomachean Ethics* with this "truth": "Every art and every investigation, and likewise every practical pursuit or undertaking, seems to aim at some good: hence it has been well said that the Good is That at which all things aim" ([335–323 B.C.] 1975, p. 3, I.i.1). For Aristotle, happiness is one's natural highest good. He used the term *eudaimonian,* which is usually translated as happiness but really means flourishing—a complete activation of one's being. It includes both "doing good" and "doing well." But can happiness be further defined? Aristotle also says that happiness is the exercise of one's *ergon,* which has been translated as one's "function" or as one's "characteristic action" ([335–323 B.C.] 1975, p. 31, I.vii.10). In other words, the kind of activity that distinguishes an agent serves as an indicator for its purpose. This definition can be used for persons as well as organizations. The purpose of the outpatient clinic, for example, would come from the kind of activity or service that provides its special identity: the activity of healing human life. It is important to note here that the purpose does not belong to the act itself but rather to the agent. Acts, in other words, do not have purposes, but moral agents do. Acts have consequences and results, but not purposes. So, when we ask, "What is the purpose of doing that?" we need to look at the purpose of the doer rather than the purpose of the act itself.

If purpose is grounded in the identity of the agent, an ethics of purpose would seem to commit the naturalistic fallacy, because it seems to derive what ought to be done from what is. This would not be true, however, if purpose does not refer to our behavior but rather to our potential as particular persons or organizations. Alasdair MacIntyre interprets Aristotle in a similar way: "Within that teleological scheme there is a fundamental contrast between man-as-he-happens-to-be and man-as-he-could-be-if-he-realized-his-essential-nature" (1981, p. 50). To move from observable behavior to potential action, we must consider not merely what we observe but also what we believe is possible. By pursuing this avenue of investigation, we not only avoid the naturalistic fallacy but also uncover our best possibilities. We can speak of what we should become according to our resources and talents. The outpatient clinic, for example, could be understood as having the resources and potential of providing quality health care. The clinic's end, therefore, would be to provide health care to patients such as Ralph who have had problems with drugs. The members' understanding of quality health care would become the criterion for evaluating what the clinic should do. The evaluation concerns what kinds of acts fit with their purpose or what means are appropriate for their end.

Central to choosing the right means is understanding the relationship between means and ends. MacIntyre's distinction between internal and external is helpful here: "I call a means internal to a given end when the end cannot be adequately characterized independently of a characterization of the means" (1981, p. 172). If we want to achieve organizational integrity, for example, then only acts of integrity would be appropriate means to achieve this end. External means, in contrast, would be means that could later be disregarded after the end is attained. I might have attainment of wealth as a purpose, for example, and since money is green no matter where it comes from — or at least some would say so — the means of attainment used would be external, not a necessary dimension of the end achieved.

Whether any means can be wholly external depends on our assumptions about how things work themselves out. Even if external means do not affect the end achieved, they do affect the person or organization that uses them. Aristotle puts it this way: "In a word, our moral dispositions are formed as a result of the corresponding activities. Hence it is incumbent on us to control the character of our activities, since on the quality of these depends the quality of our dispositions" ([335–323 b.c.] 1975, p. 75, II.1.8). If the purpose of the outpatient clinic is healing human life, then it must choose actions (means) that not only accomplish this purpose for its clients but also allow it to become a healing organization itself. What happens to this group if they decide to keep the mistake a secret? Does this secret create a climate that will hinder the clinic's future development? Can a clinic that has secrets become as good as a clinic without them? Does the health clinic itself become less healthy by engaging in such practices? The answers participants give will depend on the good they want to achieve and the kinds of persons and organizations they want to become. Setting the ethics of purpose in the decision-making diamond (as shown in Figure 12), which includes bases for observations, value judgments, and assumptions, generates the following questions as we move around the bases:

Figure 12.

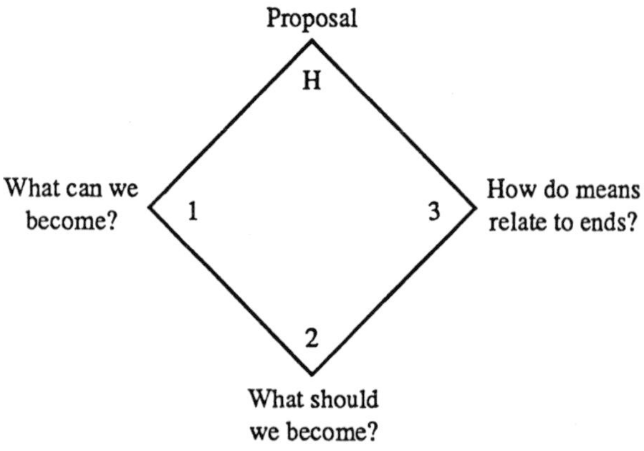

Proposal

H

What can we
become?   1   3   How do means
                                                       relate to ends?

2

What should
we become?

Base 1:   The observations focus on the potential or
          resources of the agent.

Base 2:   The value judgments interpret the highest
          potential or "characteristic action" as the
          agent's purpose.

Base 3:   Key assumptions include the relationship
          between means and ends and that agents
          should realize their potential.

Answering these questions will give us material to develop an
argument for a particular act, which will look like Figure 13.

Figure 13.

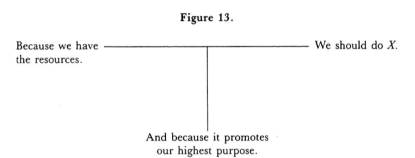

Because we have ———————————————————— We should do X.
the resources.

And because it promotes
our highest purpose.

To illustrate how the ethics of purpose guides the process of ethical reflection, and especially the interpretation of organizational
life, we can move from the particular case of the outpatient clinic
to a brief discussion of the purpose of organizations.

The Purpose of Organizations. Suppose that an enterprising person started a small leather shop in his barn. He found the best
leather and made excellent horse harnesses that were softer and
more durable than other harnesses on the market. As the demand for his products grew, he had to hire help to keep up with
the new orders. As sometimes happens, the business continued
to grow, and in a few years, he had a company with hundreds
of workers, most of whom felt some degree of identification with
the leather goods they were producing. In fact, the company
had always had a strong identity with its product: harnesses that
decreased the harshness of life for both man and beast. The

company's corporate logo was "Gentle Harnesses for Working Horses" (GHWH).

Well, things do change, and soon the introduction of the automobile wrecked the market for harnesses. The company's product had become a relic. What happened? The owner sold the company to a rubber manufacturer, who obtained new resources to make automobile tires.

As far as I know, this is not a true story, but the pattern embedded in the story has happened countless times. It begins by someone devising a "better mousetrap," followed by organizations created to provide the product. Demand for the product vanishes, and the organization finds another product to continue its existence. The pattern seems ordinary and not so unusual, but before we simply accept that that is the way things are, we need to ask what consequences this has for ethical reflection about organizational life.

The GHWH company faced a decision. What should it become? How could it decide? On one level, the company produced good harnesses, but harnesses did not have a future. On another level, the company provided employment. At yet another level, the company provided an important part of the community's industrial base. Given these different levels of interpretation, and possibly even others, our answer to the question of what the company should do will depend on how we interpret the purpose of a business. Is the purpose to (1) make a profit, (2) produce goods and services, (3) meet material and social needs, or (4) all of the above?

To understand these possibilities better, let us place GHWH next to two other organizations — a hospital and a university — and see what similarities and differences emerge. At first glance, these three seem to have different products, different clients, and different reasons for existing.

Organization	Purpose
Hospital	Provide health services
University	Provide education
Leather factory	Provide harnesses

Some may argue that a good organization provides good products (health services, education, or harnesses). Others may argue that the leather factory's purpose is not really to produce harnesses. Production is really only the means for making a profit. After all, we all know about the profit motive. Is the end production or profit? To answer this question, we need to recognize the difference between an organization's purpose and an individual's motive for investing in a company.

Do harness manufacturers or workers differ from doctors or teachers in their relationship to the organization in and through which they make a living? (The phrase *make a living* should refer to both making a life and making money. As we know from experience, the quality of our life depends on the kind of living we have made.) Certainly, many doctors and teachers have done fairly well in making a living, and yet many of us wonder about profit becoming the purpose of health care or education. We may not feel so uneasy about the profit-seeking harness company, but maybe we should. Although profit making may be a motive for individuals, it may not be the purpose of organizations.

Let us say that the individuals in these three organizations all wanted to become wealthy. We can even assume that all three organizations have stockholders who have invested their savings and pension funds for a profitable investment. We have institutions known as "for-profit hospitals" and "private" education. Each has the same responsibility to its stockholders. Does that give them the same purpose? An ethics of purpose would have us consider the characteristic action of each organization. Do these three organizations not have significantly different functions in our society? Does the clinic not still have the purpose of providing health care, the school of providing education, and the harness factory of providing good harnesses? Is not the *first* responsibility of these organizations to provide good products and services for the public?

The distinction between organizational purpose and individual motive allows us to apply an ethics of purpose to organizations and to counter those who define the bottom line as the sole criterion of corporate success. It also allows us to acknowledge that individuals may have a variety of motives for joining or running a business. Without a profit motive, many of our needed businesses probably would not exist, and without wages, much unattractive work would never get done. But these individual motives do not define the purpose of a corporation. Organizations do not have motives; people do. As we learned in Chapter Two, organizations have their own reasons for their decisions, and some of the strongest reasons appeal to an organization's mission, not to any one group's motive. At least according to an ethics of purpose, a corporation's purpose is defined by its potential, which resides in the corporation's particular employment of resources.

What are the resources? Resources are those aspects of organizational life that give an organization its end and the means to achieve that end. Resources include the organization's constituencies—workers, investors, consumers, citizens—the natural elements, and technological development. Another resource is the organizational leadership that combines and transforms these resources into the productive forces that create products and provide services as well as develops the organization itself. These resources function as means toward an end, but none of them alone defines the end. Instead, through the organizational process itself, an organization develops a "characteristic action" that defines what it is, what it does, and to what end. As the various resources change, so also does the organization's purpose. It can change from making harnesses to making tires, because of changes in resources. To allow one constituency's motives to become the organization's purpose, however, confuses the distinction between individual and corporate identity as well as the difference between means and ends.

This discussion of organizational purposes demonstrates a strength of an ethics of purpose. It allows us to ask, "What are we trying to realize?" and "Are we going about it in the right way?" These can be extremely productive questions. The weakness is that sometimes our concern for achieving a goal slights the concern for the right means. Also, sometimes the purpose seems to justify too much or too many kinds of acts. Drug testing, for example, may be a means toward a safe workplace, but it may also violate individual rights. If it does, then an organization practicing drug testing would not develop its full potential, since surely an organization that does not violate rights is superior to one that does. An ethics of purpose, however, does not always consider the quality of acts in themselves with the same concern with which it considers the notion of purpose. Since an ethics of principle focuses almost exclusively on the act itself, it can serve as a complement and even as a correction to an ethics of purpose.

Ethics of Principle

Although we sometimes evaluate a course of action by looking at what we want to achieve, at other times we consider only the character of the act itself. For example, much of the debate over investments in South Africa has focused on what purpose the withdrawal of Western multinationals from South Africa would serve. One side has argued that withdrawal would help to achieve an integrated society in South Africa. The other side has argued that withdrawal would not pressure the South African government to change. Many others, however, have not considered the question of the right means but rather have argued that cooperating with an explicitly racist state is wrong in itself. They base their argument on principle.

In using an ethics of principle, we need to know if the principles we have chosen are the right ones and why we should obey them. The nineteenth-century German philosopher Immanuel Kant addressed both of these questions. A university professor, Kant wrote in an arcane academic language that does not facilitate easy comprehension, and yet he developed a fairly straightforward ethical strategy. To see how it works, let us start with a hypothetical case and then move into Kant's terminology. Let us say you borrow one hundred dollars from me for a six-month period. At the end of the six months, you come to pay the money back, but as you walk out of your door, you encounter a United Way volunteer who asks you to make a donation for the homeless. Let us also say the people who receive help from United Way have a greater need for the hundred dollars than I do. What would you do?

Immanuel Kant would say that whatever you decided, your decision entails a moral principle. If you decided to give the money to the United Way volunteer, perhaps you acted on the principle that money should be given to those in greater need, regardless of whose money it is. If instead you decided to return it to me, you may have acted on the principle that people should repay their loans or, since you promised to pay me, that people should keep their promises.

Kant's notion of an implied principle parallels our discussion of implied value judgments in Chapter Three. Just as we learned that every prescriptive decision implies some value judgment, so Kant argues that every moral decision relies on some moral principle. But where do these moral principles originate, or, to use Kant's language, what is their "ground"? Do we discover them from experience? Kant rejects this idea because he considers human experience to be too ambiguous and incomplete. Since these principles do not come from experience, he calls them "a priori," which means "before experience." Instead of our experience causing our moral principles, which would make them generalizations from experience, they are caused by reason. Therefore, for Kant, the process of ethical reflection involves thinking about the premises that our proposed action entails. When we have formulated these premises, we can judge them by what Kant ([1785] 1964b, p. 60) calls the "supreme principle of morals": "Act only on that maxim that you can at the same time will that it should become a universal law" (p. 88).

Kant also calls this law or rule the "categorical imperative." It is categorical in the sense that it involves categories or classes of things. For example, in the argument "All persons have dignity. George is a person. Therefore, George has dignity," the categorical part is the "all" statement. It applies to all items within a class, which gives it a universal character. The imperative part refers to the principle's claim. The supreme principle of morals is a command. So, the categorical imperative is a universal moral rule that commands us to obey it. But where does this command come from? Who commands us to obey? Kant's answer is that we command ourselves. We have willed the categorical imperative; therefore, we also will to obey it.

This understanding of how the moral law comes about allows Kant to affirm human freedom. In the preface of his work, he defines ethics as the laws of freedom ([1785] 1964b, p. 55). Since every rational being engages in the same process of willing universal laws and judging whether her or his maxim conforms to them, everyone exercises the same freedom and possesses the same unqualified good — a good will. Since we have willed the moral law, we have already willed to obey it. It is our own.

Furthermore, since we are the creators of the moral law, Kant's categorical imperative applies not only to the act or policy we are considering but also to us. His second formulation of the categorical imperative addresses us as agents: "Act in such a way that you always treat humanity, whether in your own person or in the person of any other, never simply as a means, but always at the same time as an end" ([1785] 1964b, p. 96). In other words, all rational beings have the same freedom and power of legislation. They too are "ends in themselves." In another section of the *Groundwork,* Kant picks up this theme of treating people as ends in terms of price and dignity: "Therefore morality, and humanity so far as it is capable of morality, is the only thing which has dignity. Skill and diligence in work have a market price; wit, lively imagination, and humour have a fancy price; but fidelity to promises and kindness based on principle (not on instinct) have an intrinsic worth" ([1785] 1964b, p. 102). The distinction between price and dignity helps us to acknowledge that persons are ends in themselves. Persons cannot be exchanged or used solely for other purposes. Ultimately, free persons are the basis for morality.

Returning for a moment to our question about repaying the loan, an ethics of principle supplies not only the criterion of universalizing an implied moral premise or maxim but also the criterion of treating each other as ends and not merely as means. We can ask two questions: First, can you will that everyone has a duty to give money to those in greater need regardless of who the money belongs to? Or would you will that we should repay our loans? Second, does using the money to help the poor mean that you have treated the lender as only a means and not also as an end in himself? These questions reveal Kant's assumption about reasoning—namely, that it entails consistency. Reason dictates that whatever I choose for myself should also become available for others. To be consistent—to be rational—is to see one's own principle as a universal law. The inconsistency of promising one thing and then doing another so contradicts itself that it destroys the very activity of promising. Soon people will not trust each other; making promises will become impossible. In other words, in moral reasoning, there are no "special cases." To take one's own case as special is to commit the fallacy of special pleading, a fallacy based on giving yourself permissions you would not grant to others in similar situations.

Should the outpatient clinic tell Ralph about the medical mishap? Let us start our analysis by saying no. Then we will develop a maxim of this action such as: "We should not tell risky patients the truth if it might jeopardize their treatment." Can we universalize this? Can we will that everyone should not tell risky patients the truth if it might jeopardize their treatment? If you were a patient such as Ralph, would you agree that the clinic should not tell you the truth? These are the questions the categorical imperative's first formulation would have us answer.

The second formulation asks us if our proposed action really treats Ralph not only as a means but also as an end. Does it show respect for Ralph's freedom as a moral being? Some might say that withholding such information prevents Ralph from acting freely, because one cannot act freely under false assumptions. Others might argue that Ralph needs help and that not telling him helps him fulfill his plans for a drug-free life. Once we acknowledge Ralph's freedom, however, our help cannot become overly paternalistic and do what is good for him if it is against his will. It seems that the only way we can disregard Ralph's freedom is to regard him as incapacitated and incapable of moral agency.

An ethics of principle has a quite different approach than

an ethics of purpose. Instead of beginning with the natural potential of agents and finding their purpose, it begins with the principle implied in our action and then seeks to discover whether
the principle is universally valid. Placing this ethical approach
in the decision-making diamond prompts a process of ethical
reflection illustrated by Figure 14.

Figure 14.

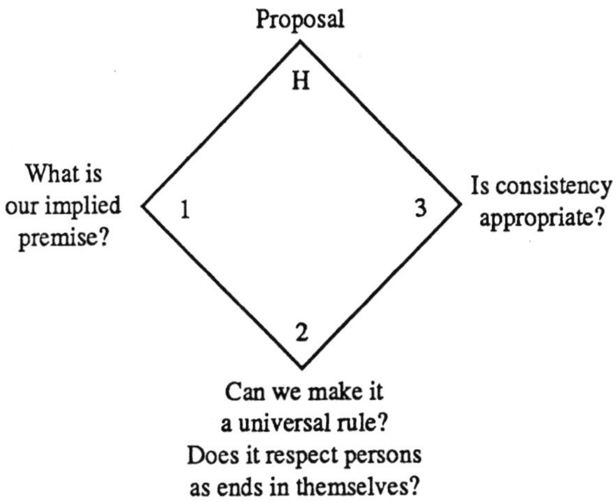

Proposal

H

What is our implied premise?

1   3

Is consistency appropriate?

2

Can we make it
a universal rule?
Does it respect persons
as ends in themselves?

Base 1:   The observations concern the implied
          moral principle of our proposed course
          of action.

Base 2:   The value judgments see if the implied
          principle can become a moral rule and
          if the act treats persons as ends — with
          respect for their dignity.

Base 3:   The key assumptions include the affirma-
          tion of consistent action and that per-
          sons are morally equal.

The answers we find through this ethical approach fit the argumentative model shown in Figure 15.

Figure 15.

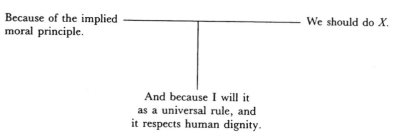

Because of the implied ———————————————————— We should do *X*.
moral principle.

And because I will it
as a universal rule, and
it respects human dignity.

An ethics of principle involves the following process of reflection. An agent proposes to do an act or institute a policy. We ask, "Why?" The response is, "Because I choose to do it." We can investigate the choice by discovering its implied moral principle or maxim. We can then ask if we think this should become a universal rule and if it respects human dignity. If so, then the act is justified.

The strength of an ethics of principle is certainly its respect for persons as moral agents, as well as its emphasis on a basic equality of human dignity. The principle of universal law ensures such equality. The weakness of this approach, however, is fairly serious, at least in some cases. An ethics of principle does not consider the consequences of actions or policies. To fill this void, we can turn to an ethics of consequence.

Ethics of Consequence

To evaluate the consequences of an act or policy, what do we need to know? We need to know the probable consequences and what they mean for those affected by them. We also need to know how the total positive consequences compare with the total negative consequences. Once we have this information, we can choose the act or policy that causes the most good and does the least harm to those involved. To understand such reasoning, we can turn to Jeremy Bentham (1748–1832) and John Stuart Mill (1806–1873), the two chief architects of utilitarianism.

The utilitarians, especially those who collaborated with

Jeremy Bentham, were known as "radical philosophers." They worked for political reform and campaigned for liberal causes such as the extension of voting rights. In contrast to the academic context of Kant's philosophy, utilitarianism lived in the realm of politics and social reform. In other words, utilitarianism began as a public ethic, and the utilitarians primarily considered an act's consequences for the total population. For the utilitarians, the only principle by which to judge actions or laws was the "greatest happiness principle," or the "principle of utility," which Bentham defines as follows: "By the principle of utility is meant that principle which approves or disapproves of every action whatsoever, according to the tendency which it appears to have to augment or diminish the happiness of the party whose interest is in question: or, what is the same thing in other words, to promote or to oppose that happiness. I say of every action whatsoever; and therefore not only of every action of a private individual, but of every measure of government" ([1781] 1961, p. 17). In other words, if a proposed action promotes happiness, then it is right; if it promotes unhappiness, it is wrong. Simple enough, and precisely what the utilitarians wanted: a simple criterion to determine "scientifically" what actions and laws should be permitted. Just as natural scientists studied natural phenomena and formulated the "laws of nature," the utilitarians wanted to observe experiences of pleasure and pain and draw conclusions about moral laws. But how do you measure pleasure and pain for different groups or individuals? This question has continued to trouble utilitarians, but Bentham thought they could be measured by such elements as their intensity, duration, certainty or uncertainty, and propinquity or remoteness ([1781] 1961, p. 37). Pleasures that were more intense, of longer duration, of greater certainty, and closer to one's home would have more value than pleasures lacking these characteristics. In fact, these categories only measure the quantity and not the quality of pleasure and pain. John Stuart Mill, as we will see, criticizes Bentham for not recognizing this difference.

The debate about the meaning of consequences for different persons largely evolved around the assumed relationship between individual and public interests. Some utilitarians thought these interests were identical, and others thought they were not. Adam Smith, the father of capitalism, believed in the identity of interests: "Every individual is continually exerting himself to find out the most advantageous employment for whatever capital he can command. It is his own advantage, indeed, and not that of society, which he has in view. But the study of his own advantage naturally or, rather, necessarily leads him to prefer that employment which is most advantageous to the society" ([1776] 1975, p. 9). If Smith is correct, then it seems that people will naturally do what they ought to do for the good of society. Pursuing one's own happiness — one's interest — naturally benefits the total community.

Jeremy Bentham affirmed another trend in British empiricism, which Elie Halévy calls the "artificial identification of interests" (1960, p. 17). This view recognizes that some individual interests may not naturally coincide with the community's interest, so people need to be persuaded or coerced, through appropriate legislation and sanctions, not to choose such interests. This gap between people's interests — what is — and public happiness — what ought to be — gives utilitarianism its normative ethical character (Harrison, 1985, p. 107). Without the gap, it would remain a descriptive ethics. The task of utilitarianism is not only to understand cause-and-effect relations but also to use this understanding to induce people to pursue those activities that promote the public happiness (Bentham, [1781] 1961, p. 17).

If we assume a difference between individual interests and public interests, so that we cannot take what we are interested in as an indication of what we should be interested in, then how do we know what the public interests should be? Bentham argues that democracy is the best means to define public happiness, because democracy is more responsive to "the greatest number" than any other form of government. And what if the majority is wrong? Bentham admits such a possibility, but he believes that in the long run the people will correct their mistakes as they learn what legislation causes more pleasure or pain (Harrison, 1985, p. 222). So the people as a whole are the final authority in defining pleasure and pain and in deciding under what laws and moral standards they should live.

Bentham's brand of utilitarianism gave reformers a method to measure the effects of current laws and practices and a way to argue for their own programs by demonstrating that they would increase pleasure and decrease pain. His utilitarianism, however, also ignored the complexity of different kinds of pleasures. For example, how should we compare the pleasure of winning a lottery with the pleasure of completing a difficult project? Which kind of pleasure should the society, through education or regulation, promote? Bentham does not give us a way to answer such questions.

John Stuart Mill, whose father belonged to the Benthamite circle, attempted to enlarge utilitarianism to include more than pain and pleasure as measurements of happiness. Mill says of Bentham, "He committed the mistake of supposing that the business part of human affairs was the whole of them; all at least that the legislator and the moralist had to do with" ([1838] 1969, p. 106). Instead of focusing so narrowly on pleasures and pains, Mill emphasized the quality of life as well. In a famous remark directed against the exclusive focus on pleasure and pain, Mill wrote, "It is better to be a human being dissatisfied than a pig satisfied; better to be Socrates dissatisfied than a fool satisfied" ([1838] 1969, p. 260). Mill stressed other aspects of life such as the dignity of the individual and the development of character. Mill saw these aspects of life, however, as enlargements of the utilitarian principle rather than as alternatives to it.

Although Mill accepted as the ultimate end the "greatest happiness for the greatest number," he also developed "secondary ends," which would serve as guides for action and could be justified by the principle of utility. In fact, these secondary ends actually became indispensable guides for understanding the primary end of utility. For example, Mill argued against what he called "the tyranny of the majority" by stating, "If all mankind minus one were of one opinion, and only one person were of the contrary opinion, mankind would be no more justified in silencing that one person, than he, if he had the power, would be justified in silencing mankind" ([1838] 1969, p. 142). How does Mill justify this statement? He argues that in the long term such regard for individual freedom will have positive consequences for society. It contributes to everyone's freedom and creates the security that allows people to speak the truth when the majority may be in error: "Mankind are greater gainers by suffering each other to live as seems good to themselves, than by compelling each to live as seems good to the rest" ([1838] 1969, p. 138). This notion of long-term consequences even allows Mill to bring Kant's universal moral principles under the utilitarian umbrella: "To give any meaning to Kant's principle, the sense put upon it must be, that we ought to shape our conduct by a rule which all rational beings might adopt *with benefit to their collective interest*" ([1838] 1969, p. 308).

Mill's expansion of utilitarianism provides us with a sophisticated view of evaluating consequences because it has room for contributions from other ethical traditions. While utilitarianism itself does not say much about respect for human dignity, for example, it can support this principle by showing its positive long-term consequences. While utilitarianism allows us to consider the consequences of our acts, the other ethical approaches can help the utilitarian determine what consequences he or she should consider.

What would a utilitarian say the outpatient clinic should do about informing Ralph of the medical mishap? The case already suggests an answer. Since Ralph's behavior has improved because of the misinformation, the consequences of not telling him appear to be good. If telling him the truth would increase the risk that he might reject the clinic's treatment, then telling him might do more harm than good. Also, considering the size of malpractice suits today, telling the truth may endanger not only the physician's career but the outpatient clinic and the hospital as well. In this case, it seems that when all the people and institutions involved are considered, telling the truth would put many at risk and probably do little good.

This first interpretation, however, may need more reflection. What happens to groups and institutions when they engage in cover-ups? What happens to the trust among the staff and the relationship between staff and physicians? What happens the next time someone makes a mistake? What kind of culture does a cover-up create? If we consider these negative consequences, they may outweigh the good effects on Ralph's condition. Furthermore, since both an ethics of purpose and an ethics of principle seemed to favor telling Ralph what happened, maybe an ethics of consequence should take a second look at both the short-term and long-term consequences for *all* the people affected. Perhaps satisfying the clinic's interest does not differ from following its purpose or universalizing the implicit principle of its action. In fact, the three different ethical approaches together may prevent any one of them from shortsightedness. Setting an ethics of consequence in the decision-making diamond generates a process of ethical reflection illustrated by Figure 16.

Figure 16.

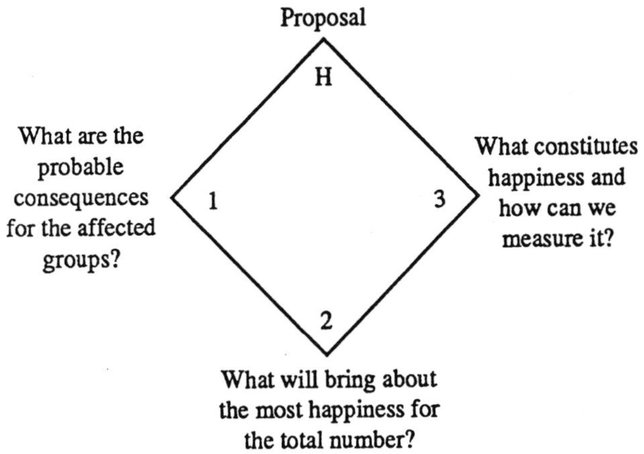

Proposal

H

What are the probable consequences for the affected groups?

1

3

What constitutes happiness and how can we measure it?

2

What will bring about the most happiness for the total number?

Base 1: The observations concern the probable consequences of a particular course of action. We need to agree first on what groups will be affected and then on what the probable consequences for these groups will be.

Base 2: The value judgments concern the greatest happiness for the total number of people involved.

Base 3: The important assumptions we need to address are the definitions of happiness (and unhappiness) and how they can be measured.

Answering these questions will give us material to develop the argument illustrated in Figure 17.

Figure 17.

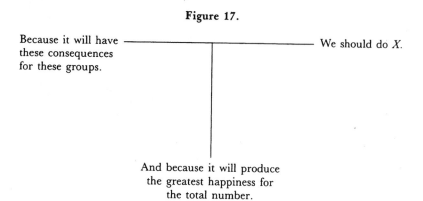

Because it will have
these consequences
for these groups.   We should do *X*.

And because it will produce
the greatest happiness for
the total number.

Linking these three ethical approaches together will show us how each one can serve as a qualification of the other. Using the part of the argumentative map that has an "unless" statement allows the following formulations:

> We should pursue our purpose unless it treats persons only as means or unless the consequences cause more harm than good.
>
> We should act on principle unless it causes more harm than good or unless it contradicts our purpose.
>
> We should do what causes the most good and least harm for all concerned unless it means treating some persons only as means and committing acts that cannot be universalized, or unless it destroys our potential to become what we should become.

As we develop these qualifications, of course, we also gain new understandings of our purposes and principles and of the consequences of our acts. The three approaches can both correct and enhance each other. They give us a comprehensive basis for dealing with disagreements about what acts can be justified, and, in many cases, they can overcome such disagreements because they include possibilities for self-correction and new knowledge. They can encourage a learning process for all participants. Furthermore, by bringing into discussions all five areas where people may disagree about human actions — act, scene, agent, agency, and purpose — they can help participants discover agreements among the five that they can leverage to overcome disagreements on the others. If people disagree about the probable consequences in the outpatient clinic case, for example, their agreement on the institution's purpose or on universal principles may prompt them to redefine the consequences. Ethical reflection, of course, cannot guarantee consensus, but at least the participants would have touched all the bases in their attempt to find the best response to the situation.

To analyze the organization and its action with these value judgments, participants can use the exercises in Chapter Eleven to integrate these ethical approaches with the argumentative map, and Table 2, in the same chapter, to examine whether all three approaches support the same course of action. If they do, then the analysis will allow decision makers to clarify many of their reasons for supporting a particular proposal. There is other information, however, that the value judgments depend upon and yet do not have the means to evaluate. Chapter Six explains how to evaluate this kind of information.

Chapter Six

Getting the Facts Straight for Reliable Decision Making

For effective decision making, you have to get your facts straight. Groups or individuals who have good intentions and even competence in using ethical concepts also need to evaluate the truth or falsity of their information. Sometimes ethical statements appear to slight the factual component of ethical reflection, and they may pay dearly for doing so. Even an ethics of principle, which depends the least on situations, still must conceive of some circumstance to formulate a proposed course of action. If the initial conceptualization is false, all else will eventually fail as well. When we use a combination of approaches, as was suggested in the previous chapter, then reliable information is essential. Policy proposals always propose actions in particular situations, and if we do not verify the facts pertinent to such situations, we may have the right value judgment but make the wrong decision. The following argument can illustrate the weakness of using only value judgments:

> We should increase our employee assistance program
> because we respect our employees.

The incompleteness of the argument becomes obvious when we place this statement in the argumentative model shown in Figure 18.

Figure 18.

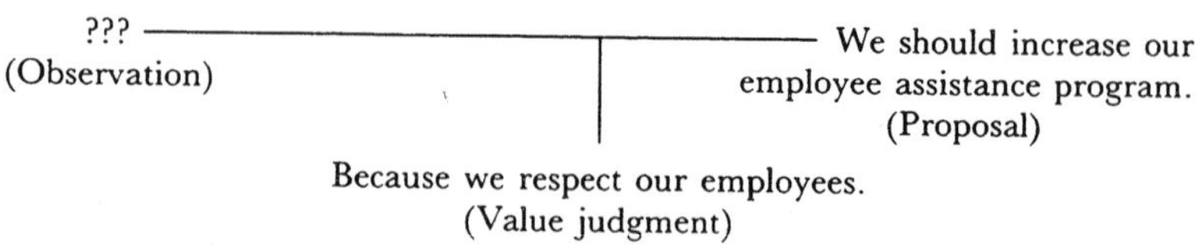

```
  ???                                                    We should increase our
(Observation)                                       employee assistance program.
                                                              (Proposal)

                  Because we respect our employees.
                         (Value judgment)
```

Let us say that everyone agrees with the value judgment. Could people still disagree with the policy? They might, because we do not know the facts of the situation. Maybe the employees' needs are currently being well served. Maybe employees want outside rather than in-house services. Perhaps people do not see any strong connection between employee assistance programs and respecting employees. Without the facts, we are at a loss to know what the policy really means. To engage in effective ethical reflection, you have to check out the facts.

Interpreted Facts

What is a fact? We so easily say, "It is a fact that . . ." Then, much to our surprise, someone disagrees. How can that happen? It happens because the kinds of facts that enter into discussions — articulated facts — are always interpreted facts. People disagree because they interpret differently. Some facts, of course, enjoy almost universal agreement, such as the "fact" that it is harder to see in the dark than in the light. (Persons who are blind might disagree even with this statement.) Many facts, however, do not enjoy such agreement. Is drug abuse alone costing American industry millions of dollars? Will ethical reflection increase organizational effectiveness? People can disagree about these facts. We could use computer terminology and speak of "hard" facts and "soft" facts. *Hard facts* would refer to data that receive universal or at least near universal assent. *Soft facts,* in contrast, would refer to data that receive only partial agreement and must be "proven" to those who disagree. To verify the facts, we need to keep in mind the characteristics of interpretation: Interpretation always originates from some perspective, always uses a particular language, and is primarily relational. Chapter Two explored the question of perspective by comparing economic, psychological, and ethical perspectives on the question of whether to involve employees in the decision of how to decrease expenses by 20 percent. These three perspectives offer not only different formulations of the issue but also different interpretations of the situation. They make different observations. The ethical perspective, like other perspectives, does not enjoy any universal stance. Only in dialogue with other perspectives and through their interaction can a group learn as much as possible. As was shown in the last chapter, the three ethical approaches taken together perform a similar service.

Interpreted facts are not only perceived from some particular perspective but also conceived with some particular vocabulary, and the terms we use color what we see. Kenneth Burke calls this our "terministic screen," which he explains this way: "When I speak of 'terministic screens,' I have particularly in mind some photographs I once saw. They were *different* photographs of the *same* objects, the difference being that they were made with different color filters. Here something so 'factual' as a photograph revealed notable distinctions in texture, and even in form, depending upon which color filter was used for the documentation description of the event being recorded" (1968, p. 45). He also warns us that "much that we take as observations about 'reality' may be but the spinning out of the possibilities implicit in our particular choice of terms" (1968, p. 46). Actually, Burke's admonition about the use of words and sets of words lies behind the distinction in Chapter Two between action and behavior, a distinction he also makes. Behaviorist terminology excludes such words as the human *will* and the notion of "free choice." Within a behaviorist framework, ethics easily becomes a means to control behavior, and only with a transformation of this perspective and terminology can we bring into view the difference between what people do (behavior) and what they decide they should do (action). When we investigate the facts, we need to evaluate the language we use for the investigation carefully.

The third characteristic of interpretation is that we usually see facts not merely as things but as things in relations. Like when learning to understand a language, we do not learn by memorizing words; we learn by understanding sentences. Words have their meanings in sentences. Objects or events also receive their significance as we relate them to other objects or events. In most of our interpretations, we use different types of relations to connect things, and some of these types have particular importance for ethical reflection.

In classical rhetoric, the relations between terms were

called *topics*, or *places*, which we can understand as the placing of terms in relationship to one another. To use the ethical approaches we learned about in the last chapter adequately and more generally to engage in the critical evaluation of information we use in the process of ethical reflection, we will have occasions when we need to analyze the following types of rhetorical topics or sets of relations: parts-whole, cause-effect, abstract-concrete, and general-specific.

An ethics of purpose depends on the truth of part-whole relations and on causal relations. Since its primary use is to choose the means that will achieve the agent's purpose, we need these topics to see whether the means actually belongs to the end (part to whole) and to know if the means will actually bring about (effect) the end the agent has chosen.

An ethics of principle requires coherent relations between concrete and abstract descriptions of events and accurate definitions of terms. Developing an implied moral principle requires an abstraction from the situation, and we need to know if this abstraction is true. Also, the analysis of the similarities and differences between different situations—the topic of comparison and contrast—can prevent us from transferring a principle from a context in which it fits to another context in which it does not.

An ethics of consequence especially depends on truthful cause-effect relations. To evaluate consequences, we have to have reliable information about what causes what or what effect an act will have. Will electric automobiles cause less air pollution or, because of the increase in electrical generation, more pollution? We need to know so that we can choose the act that will have the most positive and least negative consequences. By learning to analyze these different topics and their dangers or even fallacious use, we will increase the chance of arriving at the right decision.

Parts and Whole. The topic of parts and whole has two important functions for ethical reflection. It gives us a way to ask if the means we choose belong to the end we are trying to achieve, and it can help us understand some of the complexity of individual and collective responsibility. If we use an ethics of purpose, we can look at the means-end relationship as parallel to the part-whole relationship. The means either belongs to the end, as a part belongs to a whole, or it does not. This topic gives us another way to understand MacIntyre's distinction between internal and external means, discussed in the previous chapter. Those means that do belong to the whole would parallel MacIntyre's notion of internal means. Those that do not belong to the whole would parallel his notion of external means (1981, p. 172). In the outpatient clinic case, for example, does not telling Ralph (a part) really belong to the total practice of the clinic (the whole)? Or does the act not belong to the whole clinic's purpose? If it does not, we have a good indication about what we should do.

Belonging to a whole does not mean identify with the whole. In fact, the relationship between parts and whole may be quite complex and faces two particular hazards. One is committing the fallacy of composition, which assumes that what is true of the parts is also true of the whole. For example, a company may have a good pension plan, but that does not mean that the company as a whole is a good place to work, since much more than having a pension plan is required before the whole company is good. The opposite fallacy — the fallacy of division — assumes that what is true for the whole is true of the parts. Just because the organization has a good reputation does not mean that every department shares it.

The recent National Semiconductor case illustrates some of the complexity of part-whole thinking. The company was charged with criminal conduct in its dealings with the Defense Department. The Department of Defense argued that the individuals responsible for such conduct should be prosecuted. The company president, Charles Sporck, argued, "We totally disagree with the [Defense Department's] proposal. We have repeatedly stated that we accept responsibility as a company and we steadfastly continue to stand by that statement" (Velasquez, 1988, p. 64). Does Sporck's statement reflect the fallacy of composition? Should the activity of parts of the company be seen as activities of the whole company? Some individual employees committing fraud does not necessarily mean that the whole company is fraudulent. Whether the company is fraudulent depends on its policies and procedures, as well as their implementation. Likewise, if the company is fraudulent — its policies and procedures may actually pressure individuals into fraudulent acts as a worse evil than losing their jobs — that does not mean that all individual employees are fraudulent. As was argued in Chapter Two, both persons and organizations can be considered as moral agents. We do not need to deny the agency of one to affirm the agency of the other. The fallacies of composition and division can help us to recognize the difference between organizations and individuals, which should also prevent us from substituting one for the other.

Cause and Effect. An ethics of purpose also employs the cause-effect topic, because we need to know if the means we choose will bring about the end we desire. This topic, however, is even more fundamental for an ethics of consequence. Even more than an ethics of purpose, an ethics of consequence depends on true causal relations. Its success in producing the most good and the least harm requires that we correctly estimate an act's or a policy's consequences. It requires accurate interpretation of the effects of specific acts or activities. Steven Kerr has shown the complexity of cause-effect analysis for organizations in his article "On the Folly of Rewarding A, While Hoping for B" (1983). He argues that in some cases, even though we want to cause one kind of behavior, we set up reward systems that actually encourage another. For example, "Society *hopes* that teachers will not neglect their teaching responsibilities but *rewards* them almost entirely for research and publications" (1983, p. 116). Such confusion is not unusual. Immanuel Kant found this example amusing: "A rich heir paid his servants handsomely to cut dignified figures at the funeral of his father. But, the rascals, the more they were paid to look sad, the happier they became" (Perelman and Olbrechts-Tyteca, 1971, p. 272). These examples remind us that if we want to encourage a certain kind of action, we must be careful not to reward another.

One variation of the cause-effect topic is the topic of condition-consequence. With it, you imagine the desired consequences or effects and then construct the appropriate conditions (causes) to bring them about. For example, if you want to bring about increased employee cooperation, then you might redesign the office so that there is more interaction. Will this change in conditions actually bring about the desired consequences? The following Chinese passage (from Tai Hio, part I, no. 4) illustrates that the connections may be more complex than first imagined: "The Ancients, who desired intelligence to play its education role through the whole country, first established order in their principality; desiring to establish order in their own principality, they first regulated their family life; desiring to regulate their family life, they first improved their own characters; desiring to improve their own characters, they first purified their hearts; desiring to purify their hearts, they sought for sincerity in their thoughts; seeking for sincerity in their thoughts, they applied themselves to perfect knowledge; this perfect knowledge consists in acquiring a sense of reality" (Perelman and Olbrechts-Tyteca, 1971, p. 230).

As we think about the conditions necessary for responsible action, this passage encourages us to consider all that must be changed to really change anything at all. If we want a more cooperative organization, for example, it behooves us to consider what else we have to change besides developing a new policy statement. We will look at some of the conditions necessary for ethical reflection in Chapter Eleven, after we consider some other essential conditions such as the organization's system and its basic assumptions. Conditions by themselves, however, will not create new kinds of interactions. People must also change.

How can you know when situations have changed? Or what has caused the change? We hear of all types of changes and of how one factor changed another, but can we be sure that the reporters have gotten the facts straight? Consider the following statement:

The productivity of the department increased 8 percent after participatory management was introduced.

Although this statement may appear to present important information, some readers may remain skeptical about it, and for good reasons. An 8 percent increase does not tell us very much until we know the numbers on which it is based. If the department had been very unproductive, say producing only 10 pieces a day, then 10.8 may not signal a significant increase in productivity. If the department had already been quite productive, producing 40 pieces a day, then an 8 percent increase to 43.2 pieces could indicate a move toward full employment of its resources. We need to know more about the prior conditions before we gain reliable information from percentages.

Since we have already covered the part-whole topic, we can also raise a question about the relationship between the department and its members. The statement speaks only of the department, but what is true for the department might not be true for each worker (the fallacy of division). We do not know if each member has increased his or her work by 8 percent or if some increased their work by 30 percent and others decreased their work by 5 percent. Furthermore, we should not assume that every person, simply by virtue of being a department member, will be very productive.

Along with clarifying the significance of the 8 percent increase, we need to know more about the assumed causal relationship between participatory management and the increase in productivity. Although such a relationship is assumed, the causal connection remains unclear. The research has not accounted for other possible causes for the increase in productivity. Maybe the work force had high performance expectations from their home life or performed well because they wanted promotions. In other words, we need more evidence that participatory management caused the increased productivity. We know only that participatory management procedures and productivity both occurred at the same time. We can see a correlation between the two, but, as every student of statistical research knows, a strong correlation does not necessarily imply a causal relation.

The second form of misreading causal relations is to think that just because one event happened before another, that the first event therefore caused the second. This is the *post hoc ergo propter hoc* (after this, therefore because of this) fallacy. Examples of post hoc reasoning abound. For example, one may observe an increase in hair length among teenagers and a subsequent decrease in their scholastic grades, but this may only be a correlation without any causal significance. Or one may observe an increase in corporate crime and a subsequent increase in mortgage payments, but whether one causes the other must be proven. Proof requires that all other possible causes for the increase have been eliminated, so no other variables can account for the change. Although the introduction of worker participation may have increased productivity, simply change itself or, in effect, any change could also have caused the increase. When people present relations as causal, watch out for other factors that could have been the cause. Maybe new technology was introduced, or maybe the added attention that participatory management caused brought about the increase. Knowing what happened during the same period of time with other departments that did not use participatory management practices would help to strengthen this statement. In scientific research, people use control groups that have similar characteristics to the research group so they can rule out all factors other than the one they are studying.

Another risk in using the cause-and-effect topic is that of confusing a symptom for a cause. For example, is drug abuse a cause of low morale and low productivity in the workplace, or is it a symptom? Do we find less drug abuse in interesting and productive work environments? Perhaps drug abuse manifests individual and social conditions rather than causing these conditions. Perhaps we are dealing with symptoms or with correlations — people who have low self-esteem, are careless, and work in unproductive workplaces sometimes use drugs and sometimes have accidents. If so, then we may also be ignoring factors other than drug abuse that have strong causal force.

Our assumptions about cause-effect relations shape much of our information about organizational life and what we should do. The information alone cannot tell us what to do, but when we supply the appropriate value judgments, our assumptions become very important. In many cases, our causal statements are based on generalization from specific incidences or experiences, and then we argue for specific causal connections from these generalizations. For example, we could argue that ethical reflection increases organizational effectiveness. This is a statement about causes, and we can support it with other causal statements such as: (1) ethical reflection increases resources for decision making, and (2) increased resources will enable better decisions, which in turn will increase organizational effectiveness. This is an argument about the facts, and its strength depends on the evidence we can find to support it. Such evidence can include specific examples, which support generalizations. To have confidence in generalizations, we need to know some of their hazards.

Generalizations and Specifics. The general-specific topic takes single or multiple instances and makes a generalized statement from the instances. Generalizations are statements *from* a number of instances *about* all such instances. For example, if we observe that in our organization the college graduates ask more questions about strategic planning than those without a college education, then we may generalize that a college education produces a more questioning work force. (Actually, this group may have been more questioning even without a college education.)

People disagree with generalizations for a number of reasons. Sometimes the generalization simply does not have enough instances to support it. This is called a hasty generalization. Another kind of faulty generalization consists of statements that say more than the instances really allow, which sometimes happens when we generalize from our own personal experience. Although you may have learned much from one experience, the experience remains only one example and, as with other examples, other people can refute it by counterexamples. Also, our experience "belongs" to its own particular situation. To apply its learning outcome to another situation, unless clearly similar, may leave one caught in an old answer that ignores new information. Still, most learning does come from experience, and you can move from experience to convincing generalizations by submitting the experience to group discussion. You can allow others to review your story or see if other generalizations conform equally well to your experience. Refusing to let others examine the "evidence," or in this case to let them hear the story, surely increases the risk of making a faulty generalization.

Sometimes a story can take on mythic proportions in the sense that it gives such a closed and complete identity to an individual or a group that they cannot move outside of the story. Caught in their own history, they cannot respond to new circumstances. While stories give us an identity and even a framework for understanding current events, they can also narrow our vision if they are stories that already have an end when we must continue to live in an unfinished world.

Most series of events, of course, have more than one story. Vietnam veterans tell a different story about the Vietnam War than do civilians. Parents tell a different story than do soldiers. Vietnamese tell a different story than do Americans. What is the "real" story? That is hard to say, but we can at least allow for a composite story rather than a single one. We need to ask of each telling: "Who's telling it?" "Who's included in and who's left out of the story?" "Why is it being told?" "What are the other versions?" In many settings, of course, stories have an integrity of their own, and analysis seems inappropriate. In the process of ethical reflection, however, we need to articulate the point of the story and bring the point into the discussion, so that participants can analyze its message. A story's message always says more than the story itself because the message may explain other situations. Whether the message does have such explanatory power depends on its implicit value judgments and assumptions, which can only be discovered when the message becomes part of the whole process of ethical reflection. Generalizations are necessary for ethical reflection, and yet they also may block such reflection if they are not presented as candidates for analysis to make sure they are not saying too much. Whereas a generalization usually says more than the particular instances, another topic—the abstract-concrete—always says less. At the same time, the process of abstraction is endemic to reflection.

Abstract and Concrete. All critical thought involves abstracting, a drawing away from lived reality. But we also can place abstractions on abstractions, and while this upward movement may be fitting, it can also make us lose any connection with what actually is happening. Although we always select some aspects of a situation and ignore others, what we select should be recognized as only a part of the whole. The process of selecting and then conceptualizing the meaning of what we have selected is especially important for an ethics of principle. I may describe an experience as (1) a throbbing sensation in the forehead, (2) a headache, (3) stress, or (4) an occupational health problem. If I want to get immediate relief, it is probably better to stay at levels 1 and 2. Medication or relaxing exercises can deal with headaches and stress. If my supervisor approaches me, I may want to talk on level 4. This could mean that instead of just giving me an aspirin, management might decide to make some changes in the workplace so I will not get this throbbing sensation next week. Seeing headaches as occupational health problems may begin an exploration of how technology or the work situation contributes to illness, whereas remaining at the "headache" level may lead to no other solution than the one we bring with us: "Take two aspirin and go to bed."

Perelman and Olbrechts-Tyteca (1971, p. 121) provide a good example of abstracting from a concrete activity: "The same process can indeed be described as the action of tightening a bolt, assembling a vehicle, earning a living, or helping the export drive." The first level may appear most concrete, but it still does not mention the room temperature, the muscle movement, or the thinking process. The most abstract level—helping the export trade—in contrast, places the description in a very broad circumference. If the supervisor asks the mechanic what she is doing and receives the answer, "I am helping the export trade," the supervisor may wonder if the mechanic knows her job. On the other hand, if the mechanic speaks at a rally for trade protection, she may describe her work at that level of abstraction. The proper level of abstraction depends on the situation.

The process of abstraction is especially important for an ethics of principle in the formulation of an implied principle of a proposed act. For example, in discussions about affirmative action policies, how we formulate the implied principle will determine whether or not an ethics of principle can justify the policy. If we state the implied principle as "we should choose a member of an underrepresented group over a member of an overrepresented group until the composition of our work force matches the composition of the larger community," we may be able to will that this become a universal law. But this is a fairly abstract statement. What happens when a manager says, "I should promote Linda over Harry because Linda belongs to an underrepresented group"? In the actual situation, we may find that abstracting the gender difference between Linda and Harry actually omits too many other concrete details, such as Harry's ten years with the company, their different personalities, and so on. Soon we have all the details, but no direction. We have moved to a level of abstraction where selecting one individual over another on the basis of gender seems rather odd. Perhaps the whole process of selection seems odd. For affirmative action policies to make good sense, we need to approach them at the proper level of abstraction.

Another voice may ask us to justify the statement that "Harry should not be promoted because he belongs to an over-represented group." Could we justify that statement? Some have seen this as "reverse discrimination." But their term *reverse discrimination* demonstrates how an abstraction can overlook relevant concrete differences. Discrimination against persons because of their race or sex, which has been linked with racist and sexist attitudes, differs substantially from discrimination based on an oversupply. If the concrete situation from which the term *discrimination* received its meaning is not clarified, the term loses its connection to reality and becomes a kind of buzzword. Abstract words have meaning if they can give thought to experience. When they unthinkingly cover up experience, we need to ask what kinds of situations and experiences the speaker has in mind.

Comparison and Contrast. All three ethical approaches can profit from the topic of comparison and contrast, because only by seeing the similarities and differences between different situations can we know when policies from old situations can also fit new ones. This topic allows us to transfer our knowledge or our attitude from the known to the unknown: "This reminds me of the time . . ." "He is just like . . ." or "That is just like what happened at our office." You can test these comparisons by making sure that the similarity in the two situations permits transfer of a particular notion from one to the other. For example, the statement "Teaching is like selling cars" rests on the similarity of the use of persuasion in each, but it ignores the differences in goals and content and community relations. Much organizational research today uses comparison and contrast to draw out the significance of its findings. If we know that a well-trained department produced eighty units a day, we do not know very much. If we also know that a similar group that did not receive the training produced sixty units, then we know much more. Most researchers attain reliable information by comparing what happens in an experimental group and in a control group. Two groups with similar characteristics are selected, and then one group, for example, is given an experimental drug and the other a placebo. The group members do not know what they received. To the extent possible, the only variable is the drug. In most settings outside of laboratories, it is difficult to control the many possible variables, so results are also less secure. Still, we can find many correlations, but remember that statistical relations do not demonstrate causal relations, only correlations.

When we use the various topics we have covered in this chapter, we usually think of one-way relationships—how *A* is related to *B*. Sometimes, we observe two-way—or reciprocal—relationships. These kinds of relations have been described as systems. In a system, *A* relates to *B*, which in turn responds to *A*, which changes *A*'s relationship to *B*, which has also been changed by *A*'s first response. Instead of an action, of *A* on *B*, we observe the interaction of *A* and *B*. In other words, the relationship is cyclical rather than causal. This interaction, furthermore, defines much of the identity of *A* and *B;* they become part of the relationship between them; they become part of the system. Organizations function like this, and in the next chapter we will pursue a systems approach to organizations and organizational issues.

The different topics we have covered here do not include all the ways we can relate things to each other but do include some we usually use. By gaining skills in recognizing and using them, we can understand the facts, as well as prevent misunderstandings. Since the facts never speak for themselves, we need to carefully consider what we encourage the facts to say through our interpretation. We can almost always interpret in more than one way, so to gain the most resources for making decisions, it helps to take a pluralistic view of interpretation. The right tools to analyze factual statements increase the possibility of making the right decision.

Chapter Seven

Managing Systems of Power and Corporate Relationships

To get ethics to work in organizations, sometimes you have to consider the organization's system or the organization as part of larger social and economic systems. If you do not, your ethical choices may do more harm than good, as the following dilemma demonstrates.

> I work for an international construction company that secures most of its work through competitive bidding. When bidding for work, many competing firms use a strategy called "shopping the job." This involves telling certain subcontractors and material suppliers that their quotations are not low enough, based on the prices submitted so far. Favored contractors are informed about other prices received and are given the opportunity to lower their prices. My company does not shop jobs because it is dishonest. As a result, we have lost jobs to other construction companies that do. If we continue to refuse, soon we will not have enough work for our employees. If we begin job shopping, then we will lose our reputation of honesty—one of the foundation stones of the company's identity.

The company's dilemma is that whatever it does will not stop the practice of job shopping. Like the basketball player who did not want to steal the opponent's ball, if the company refuses to job shop, it harms itself and aids those that do job shop; if the company does job shop, it violates its principles. If it wants to change its conduct effectively, it must change the conduct of the whole system. In other words, only by establishing a fair and just system can it exercise its right to do what is right.

Actually, we find many instances where we have to change the whole system if we want to change anything at all. If we had continued the discussion of participatory management begun in Chapter Six, for example, and concluded that workers should have more control over the management of their workplace, we would have to change the organizational systems of information, communication, decision making, and so on to carry out our decision. Without these changes, attempts to engage workers in accepting more management responsibility without the resources that reside in the various organizational systems would certainly fail.

We also find instances where a systems approach increases our understanding of the actual sets of relations between groups and institutions. In our discussion of constituency representation on corporate boards, for example, we developed a management argument that constituencies should not sit on boards because they are outsiders. As long as we view these different groups as separated units, with their own interests and bases of power, then the notion of outsiders and insiders seems appropriate, even though it quickly turns the argument into insolvable conflicts of interests and power. As shown in Chapter Three, to continue this debate, we really need to use a systems perspective to interpret power relations. If we define a system as "sets of components that work together for the overall objective of the whole" (Churchman, 1968, p. 11), then the constituencies become components of the whole system. In fact, we can view corporations as belonging to larger systems or as a system, depending on our focus. Likewise, groups within a corporation may be seen as a system or a subsystem. If corporate management and a corporation's constituency are part of the same system, then the inside-outside terminology becomes unsuitable. Instead, we have different entities inside other entities or subsystems within systems. Instead of picturing the constituencies as outside of corporate circles, a systems approach encourages us to picture the corporation as inside the circle of the constituencies, and even the constituencies as inside the circle of the larger society. There is no outside but only insides, with individuals, groups, corporations enveloped by ever-widening circles.

If the corporation exists in encompassing circles, then why not have representatives from these circles on its board? If there is no outside, then constituencies can also develop a variety of ways to influence the corporation, even from various activities within its own circles. As we think about relationships between different groups or entities, a systems perspective allows us to understand their mutually interdependent relationships.

In a sense, we all know this. The term *system* has become part of our everyday language, and, for many, a systems perspective has become almost taken for granted. Current debates about the destruction of the rain forest or the greenhouse effect presuppose a systems approach. The pictures of our planet from outer space have also given us a new awareness of how we ultimately depend on one another. Today, many of us recognize that all organizations must take into account the future of the whole planet. Much of this concern has arisen from the discovery of the limits of the ecological system and the fear that we will destroy the very environment on which we ultimately depend. These fears are probably well founded, but this understanding of systems should not be automatically transferred to human systems. Whereas we must respect the basic design of the ecological system — its intricate sets of relations — the designs of human systems are human creations and can be changed. Furthermore, whereas our ecological system is essentially a closed system, human systems are open. We can grasp the significance of this difference by reviewing some central concepts of open systems theory in terms of organizational systems. Then we will translate these concepts into concepts of organizational power, so that we can understand the requirements for managing systems. This will give us the basis for demonstrating how justice and rights should be used as guides for managing systems of power.

Organizations as Systems

In a closed system, the sources for the dynamics of the system are basically within the system itself. When such a system depletes its sources of energy, there is no replacement, as we are discovering with the depletion of many natural resources. Human systems, in contrast, obtain resources from the environment. In systems terminology, human systems engage in a cyclical process of input, transformation, and output: "In a factory the raw materials and the human labor are the energic input, the patterned activities of production, the transformation of energy, and the finished product the output. Maintaining this patterned activity requires a continued renewal of the inflow of energy. This is guaranteed in social systems by the energic return from the product or outcome" (Katz and Kahn, 1978, p. 20). Open systems theory, in other words, views organizations as energy systems: "For human organizations, as for other open systems, the basic systemic processes are energic and involve the flow, transformation, and exchange of energy" (Katz and Kahn, 1978, p. 753). The sources of this energy (input) are natural resources, technology, and the organizations' various constituencies. Consumers, investors, workers, and managers all provide input into the system. The system's own process of transformation then distributes this energy according to its structures of production and maintenance. Since the products and services (output) continually require new resources (input), organizational systems depend on the environment and the continued contributions of various constituencies for survival.

What does this mean for corporate constituencies? It shows us that the constituencies provide the energy necessary for a corporate system. When they ask for representation, they are not asking to become part of a system that they do not belong to. From a systems perspective, there are no outsiders. After we place constituencies within the whole system, we still must determine their relationship with the organization. Some may argue that we should interpret systems of productive organizations and their constituencies from an economic perspective. The basic relationships, then, are relations of exchange, and we can use economic models to show how the exchanges work. Although this model certainly has some advantages for specific aspects of management, it tends to assume a closed rather than an open system, which humans can change. To understand how we can change organizational systems, we need to know more about open systems theory.

Central to the open systems theory are the concepts of entropy and negative entropy. Open systems theory "begins with the concept of entropy, the assumption that without continued inputs any system soon runs down" (Katz and Kahn, 1978, p. 3). The principle of entropy means that every transformation loses energy. If systems are not replenished—if they do not receive more input than output—they eventually grind to a halt. We experience entropy in all human systems, even in personal relations, as many of us know. Change and renewal become necessary just to keep even. Negative entropy is the reversal of this energy loss. It occurs either through new inputs to the system or through certain activities that produce a gain that overcomes any loss. For example, teaching entails a transformation of energy, but because teachers do not lose the information they share and the students gain it, there is a net gain. Learning is a win-win situation and a good example of negative entropy. Even with the possibilities of internal negative entropy, the principle of entropy can help us understand an organization's tendency for growth and expansion.

Growth is the other side of an organization's vulnerability to losing energy. In other words, the notion of entropy confirms our suspicion that things cannot remain the same; they either grow or decline. To ward off the threat of decline, organizations need to grow. Growth and development belong to the very dynamics of survival. Organizations need to get more out of resources than they put into them, which is possible as long as the whole has a creative power that is greater than its parts. This depends on several factors, of course, but not least among them is that organizations become vital, learning, and innovative systems of change, because these kinds of activities counter entropy without depleting existing resources. Without this dynamism, an organization's need for renewal will drive it to overstate its case for control. The concept of a system's "steady state" can help us understand this reaction.

Steady state refers to the phenomenon that systems tend to maintain a balance or equilibrium among the different parts of the system. When one part of the system changes, the other parts tend to compensate, so that the system itself remains the same. This could also be called a system's dialectical character. As one part of the system moves in a certain direction, another part moves in the opposite direction as a way of maintaining the system's equilibrium. For example, in a family system, as the teenager becomes more "rebellious," the parents become more authoritarian or controlling. One movement, in other words, projects its opposite. You can see the dialectic in the dynamics of growth. As systems grow, they move toward the multiplication and specialization of tasks and roles, or differentiation, and this change creates the need for a countermove for greater coordination and strategies for maintaining cohesiveness throughout the system (Katz and Kahn, 1978, p. 29). The differentiation brings about an increased need for coordination and, according to Katz and Kahn, "an over determination of the behavior necessary to preserve the organization" (1978, p. 47). Rather than merely bringing in enough energy to counteract entropy, organizations tend to bring in a surplus to further their growth and development (Katz and Kahn, 1978, p. 27). Just as the need to counter entropy leads to an expansion beyond mere replacement of energy, so also does increased differentiation lead to an excess of coordination and control.

Some would like to use the notion of steady state as a reason for treating human systems as closed systems. Actually, human systems do sometimes function like closed systems, at least at first glance. For example, the recent changes in the "threat of communism" have radically changed the United States defense system, or what has been called the military-industrial complex. As changes continue to take place in eastern Europe, we notice how essential the "enemy" was for the total system. In fact, some have tried to find new enemies so that the system itself will not have to change. While this may be interpreted as "how the system works," it is also how some persons and groups manage the system. The dynamics of systems, in other words, represent tendencies, not predetermined destinies. Understanding the tendencies of human systems can help us manage them. In fact, understanding systems maintenance is just as important as understanding systems production.

Systems Maintenance

Systems not only spend energy transforming inputs into outputs in their exchanges with the environment; they also spend energy in maintaining and changing the system itself (Katz and Kahn, 1978, p. 40). Different kinds of systems, of course, require different types of maintenance, and yet all human systems have maintenance components that, like production components, must undergo the process of entropy. Therefore, these human systems also require continual negative entropy to maintain a vital system. According to Katz and Kahn the three major factors that hold systems together are (1) the functional interdependence of roles, (2) the normative requirements of these roles, and (3) the values that support the objectives of the system (1978, p. 44). Role norms, such as what it means to do a "good job," and values, such as the significance of one's work or the social meaning of one's organization, help create the energy needed to function in one's organizational role.

These integration factors are only part of the total strategies available for preserving the system. Kenneth Boulding offers three maintenance factors, or what he calls "organizers," of systems: threat, exchange, and integration (1970, p. 232). The threat system keeps things in order by saying, "You do something nice to me, or I will do something nasty to you." The exchange system is based on interactions where everyone gets what they want: "You get what you want if I get what I want." The integrative system moves beyond satisfying diverse interests to developing shared common interests and a sense of the common good: "What you want, I want." Boulding believes that these three subsystems operate in all social systems and that managers must find the best balance among them.

To see how we can apply these three organizers to a systems problem, we can return to the job-shopping case presented earlier. In this case, the system of exchange appears to have so deteriorated that bidders and sellers cannot trust each other. Those who give an initial bid do not know if their bid will be used to obtain lower bids, and other bidders do not know if the buyer has been honest in telling them of a lower bid. Restoring honest and fair practices means that everyone has to agree to keep bids secret, but this depends on trust, and trust depends on people sharing common values, which requires an activation of the integration system. In other words, the exchange system requires a strong integrative system to ensure that people will engage in "fair dealing." We could resolve the job-shopping dilemma by increasing the integrative system, which may require us to engage in conferences with the parties involved so they have opportunities to develop a stronger sense of their mutual and common interests. Or, instead of trying to revitalize the integrative system, we could enlist a stronger system of threat or control, so that contractors would not job shop for fear of punishment. We could also levy heavy fines on those who practice such dishonest practices. Many government regulations of corporate activities use the threat system. Fines, or at least the threat of legal action, have forced some corporations to decrease their pollution of the environment, to provide safe workplaces, and to produce safe products. The system of threat from and within organizations, however, has severe limitations, especially when used extensively, because it actually undermines the possibilities of social integration and promotes defensive reactions, which tend to shut down an organization's or an individual's power. Still, threat does have a place, but only within the context of the other two subsystems of integration and exchange. By itself, threat always represents some form of tyranny. Actually, how the three system organizers should be balanced will depend in part on the particular organization and in part on basic assumptions about the dynamics of human communities.

These systems organizers can help us understand the corporate management's response to their constituencies' request for representation on corporate boards. If the managers interpret the constituencies' approach as a threat, they will probably view it as a conflict of power. If they interpret it as belonging to the subsystem of integration, they will probably interpret it as a consolidation of power. In other words, how one interprets changes in the maintenance of systems can also indicate how one views power relations. In fact, the management of power and the management of systems have striking parallels.

In his analysis of power, J. K. Galbraith delineates three sources of power: personality, property, and organization (1983, p. 6). Personality power resides in great leaders, property power resides in wealth, and organization power resides in the organization itself—it arises out of the organizational system. Although both personality and property function as powers in organizations, Galbraith argues that neither one is the characteristic power of organizations (1983, p. 43). Organizing itself is an organization's power source. We could also see it as the organization's transformational processes. Organizational power belongs to the organization. Parallel to these three sources of power, Galbraith develops three instruments of power: condign (the power of punishment), compensatory (the power of exchange), and conditioned (the power of belief) (1983, p. 4). The instrument of punishment is related to personality power. The instrument of exchange is related to property power, and the instrument of conditioned belief is related to the power of organizations.

Galbraith's discussion of the sources and instruments of power helps us understand the relationship between the input of constituencies and of organizations. While the constituencies provide some essential resources for the organization, they do not exactly provide the power. The power is generated from the organizing of the resources or, in systems language, from the transformative processes and the coordination of human resources. The power of the whole organization is more than that of its parts. At the same time, this power certainly requires the continual input of resources and so, in an indirect way, faces the same threat of entropy as the system itself. This means that power is essentially dynamic and not static. It too faces entropy and needs replacement. Furthermore, organizations cannot easily relinquish power, nor can they allow its depletion. Power is the basis for their survival. So, while constituencies may not directly give power to organizations, they can certainly disempower it by withdrawing.

The parallel dynamics of systems and power also applies to the roles and relations within organizations. Whether individuals and groups have power largely depends on the design of an organization's system and its various subsystems. The organization's system, in fact, is the primary generator and distributor of power. Even though we experience the effects of having or not having power in our organizational roles or from others in their roles, power in organizations does not ultimately belong to persons but to the roles and even more to the sets of relations among the roles. These sets of relations comprise the different subsystems of the organization, which together comprise the organization itself. So, when workers ask for changes in the system to gain the resources necessary for responsible work, they are asking for power. This power, however, belongs ultimately to the organization itself and not to any persons who might occupy "powerful" roles. How the power is distributed should depend on other criteria than who currently occupies specific organizational roles.

A final parallel between the dynamics of systems and the dynamics of power is their common tendency toward excesses, which has been well recognized in discussions of power. Just as systems tend toward surpluses to ward off the threat of depletion, power tends toward more power to ward off the threat of withdrawal by those who consent to established power relations. Because excessive power usually leads to moral failure, the ethical standards of rights and justice actually belong to an organization's set of survival tools. Without them, organizations as systems of power will almost inevitably become tyrannical. At the same time, we need to acknowledge the significance of power in organizations. Power can empower persons and groups. Whether it does so depends on the management of systems. The managment of power parallels the management of systems, as the following parallels between Boulding's system organizers and Galbraith's instruments of power show:

Boulding's organizers	*Galbraith's instruments of power*
Threat	Condign (power of punishment)
Exchange	Compensatory (power of exchange)
Integration	Conditioned (power of belief)

The parallels between Boulding's concepts and Galbraith's instruments of power help us recognize that systems maintenance is more than just keeping a system running or growing. It is also a means of taking resources (input) and then distributing them first within the system (the transformation process) and then beyond the system (output). This process also distributes power. Furthermore, Galbraith's conditioned power (the power of belief) — which parallels Boulding's organizer of integration — would support the view that the integration organizer is the most important for organizational life. Without some form of integration or common belief, organizations cannot survive. This observation gives ethical reflection a further task in systems maintenance — namely, to discover and evaluate the beliefs that maintain organizations. As we have learned in earlier chapters, ethical reflection can reveal what kinds of beliefs groups rely on in the process of decision making. Ethical reflection can also ask questions about these beliefs. A pivotal question concerns how the instruments of power should be used and how to balance the system organizers. The answer finally depends on our views of organizational justice and employee rights, which Chapter Eight explores. We can learn something about the wrong use of power, however, by analyzing organizational power itself.

Organizational Power

As we have seen, Galbraith argues that the primary source of an organization's power resides in the organization itself — it belongs to the organizational system (1983, p. 6). Since organizational power is always embedded in particular structures, we do experience power through the activities of particular persons or groups, and in many cases we experience it as conflict between individuals and groups within and outside of organizations. Also, since organizational power resides in the different components of the organization, individuals can gain control over these components and thereby appropriate the system's power for themselves. Rosabeth Moss Kanter's analysis of power in organizations gives some examples of the subsystems and components that can yield power to individuals and groups: "*information* (data, technical knowledge, political intelligence, expertise); *resources* (funds, materials, space, time); and *support* (endorsement, backing, approval, legitimacy)" (1983, p. 158). Gareth Morgan (1986, p. 159) offers an even more detailed list of sources of power within an organization:

Sources of power in organizations

1. Formal authority
2. Control of scarce resources
3. Use of organizational structure, rules, and regulations
4. Control of decision processes
5. Control of knowledge and information
6. Control of boundaries
7. Ability to cope with uncertainty
8. Control of technology
9. Interpersonal alliances, networks, and control of informal organization
10. Control of counter organization
11. Symbolism and the management of meaning
12. Gender and the management of gender relations
13. Structural factors that define the stage of action
14. The power one already has

All sources in this list finally rely on controlling some part of the system's energy or its components. Persons who have control over the resources, of course, have the possibility of taking on the resources' power. Galbraith sees the leaders of large organizations as largely organizational creations and as "synthetic" personalities: "Divorced from the organization, the synthetic personality dissolves, and the individual behind it disappears into the innocuous obscurity for which his real personality intended him" (1983, p. 43). The danger, if not fate, of organizational persons is that they live in the illusion of owning things rather than in the reality that they are a part of things. Workers asking for more control in their workplace must also ask for change in the organizational system and power relations. Workers should not, however, control this power only for themselves, as their property, but for the whole organization.

If the power of organizations resides in the dynamics of the organization itself, can we establish a systems imperative for empowering organizations? To answer this question, let us examine the following case about using temporary employees in a city administration of a midsized California city:

> The city I work for has a policy of hiring temporary employees and recently decided to increase its temporary work force. Broadly defined, temporary employees do not have normal job benefits, and they may be terminated at any time without reason. Although they may join the union, they fear termination if they do. Our high employee turnover indicates that the city provides few incentives to stay or to invest in one's work. In fact, we have few long-term employees, which indicates minimal personnel resources. The city does not spend time or money training and developing temporary employees because it does not expect a good return on such an investment. At the same time, the city boasts of saving thousands of dollars by not providing temps with employee benefits. It also argues that it hires only personnel it actually needs. This attitude, however, does not give employees much incentive to contribute years of experience to the city. In fact, the lack of training and personnel development is beginning to pose serious problems. Currently, there are just barely enough experienced employees to perform the required tasks. As these people retire or leave, and if temporaries replace them, then not only will city services decline but the discontent among temporaries will most likely spread to permanent employees, which could cause major labor problems. In that case, the thousands

of dollars the city saves on the temporary program
may well be needed to defray the costs of a variety
of potential legal actions, involving temporaries or
concerning unfair labor practices.

What went wrong in this case, and why? If we look at
this situation in terms of organizational power, we see that the
hiring of temporary employees entails a disempowering not only
of the temporary and permanent employees but also of the organization itself. Those in power appear blind to the real source
of their power, which is the organization itself. Disempowering the organization, of course, does not necessarily mean that
top management will lose their power, but it does mean that
the organizational system will become dysfunctional and not
achieve its goals. Perhaps the city managers assume that their
power is like the power of property, which they can use to make
the best exchanges of wages for work. However popular this
view was in the previous century or is today, it ignores the essential fact that an organized work force (employees and managers alike) generates its power through cooperative endeavors.
Using temporary employees as described in this case is like trying to run an organization without becoming one. Becoming
an organization, on the other hand, would involve the empowerment of all members, because the organization as a whole serves
as the basis for its power.

Many organizations have recognized the importance of
employees feeling empowered by their company and this recognition has led to various types of employee participation in decision making. When these changes are primarily limited to
changes in tone and attitudes rather than in the organization's
system of power generation and control, they need to answer
to Robert Howard's analysis: "When managerial control becomes
'personalized,' the relationship of workers to the corporation is
understood in exclusively psychological and individual terms.
The very idea of power and control becomes purely therapeu-
tic, a matter of feeling rather than action. And the genuine
conflicts of working life — and, indeed, of all social life — them-

selves become personalized, dismissed as matters of mere individual preference or, worse, social deviance, rather than recognized as legitimate subjects of social and political choice" (1985, p. 120). If we take seriously that organizational power is primarily a systems product, then changes in organizational etiquette will not serve as a substitute for organizational ethics.

When we look at the actual relations between persons and between groups in organizations, we can interpret these relations in terms of who has how much influence over what and over whom. In other words, we can look at power relations. We can even interpret the relations between organizations and their environments in similar terms. A description of the power relations, and even a description of how persons attain or fail to attain power, however, tells us very little about how organizational power should be employed. An organization's purpose and criteria of effectiveness and efficiency certainly give us some standards, as does the sociopsychological dynamics of power and powerlessness, such as Kanter (1977) has described in her work on the study of women in organizations. These largely descriptive analyses, however, do not yield normative criteria for judging how power should be used. Even a powerful organization that is energetic, productive, and innovative cannot use its power to discover the right thing to do.

While a theory of organizational power does provide a kind of negative standard for systems maintenance, it cannot finally give an organization a clear purpose or direction. Understanding systems of power can help us avoid shutting down an organization's internal and external constituencies and can help us design systems that empower rather than disempower workers, consumers, investors, and managers. But a description of how power works or what effect it has cannot tell us what kind of systems organizations should design. Once again, descriptions cannot yield prescriptions. We cannot derive what ought to happen from what is happening. Therefore, we must turn to the normative ethical criteria of justice and rights.

Effectively managing power relations is necessary for responsible organizations, but power does not have any special self-guidance system. Organizational power requires the guides of justice and rights to prevent it from doing harm and overextending itself. In our Western tradition, the most familiar constraint on the use of power has been the assertion of human rights, and these rights, in turn, have relied on just institutions for their recognition and protection. To engage in ethical analysis of organizational systems, we need to know what kinds of rights and justice are appropriate for modern organizations and especially for large corporations.

Chapter Eight

Exploring Inequalities of Justice and Rights

In the previous chapter we learned that organizations should be designed so that they empower rather than disempower their members and constituencies. Because power by itself does not include any ethical standards for its appropriate use, we also learned that the ethical standards of rights and justice are necessary for the responsible management of power. Justice does not mean that everyone deserves the same portion of power. The dynamics of systems, its growth through differentiation and coordination, continually creates new differences among persons. The multiplication of roles, relations, and responsibilities means that systems by their very nature are systems of differences or, we could also say, systems of inequality. In most organizations, members have different degrees of access to organizational power, depending on their roles and relations. These differences have given some people rights that others have not enjoyed. Not everyone has the right to the same salary, for example, or the same degree of responsibility or accountability. What rights people do have is sometimes confusing. Managers seem to have the right to decide whether to test workers for drugs, but we have not heard of workers talking as though they had the right to test managers for drug or alcohol use. In plant closures, top managers have asserted their "right" to "golden parachutes" while laborers lose their jobs. Can these and other differences be justified?

Some inequalities in organizations might be justified as the most efficient means of getting the work done, but this standard has less guiding power than one might expect. Slavery certainly got the work done, and so will other forms of morally outrageous oppression. So, while getting the work done is certainly a necessary condition for productive organizations, it does not provide a sufficient criterion for determining how to get it done, nor can it automatically justify the vast array of differences we experience in organizational life. Any sufficient criterion must take into account not only the organization's system of production but also an organization's moral community. Actually, it is the relationship between these two aspects of organizational life that provides the possibilities for a responsible organization.

Organizational systems and organizational communities are not really two distinct realities but rather two interpretations of organizational life. When we look at organizations from a systems perspective, we see sets of relations that function together for achieving the system's objectives. When we look at organizations from an ethical perspective, we see a moral community. A moral community is also a set of relations, but these relations are not only functional but also substantial—the moral substance that unites organizational members.

To keep organizational systems "on the right track," the system must be managed so that the system's structuring of roles and relations has some positive correspondence to the moral community's requirements for social justice and individual rights. In other words, the system's generation and distribution of power must match the community's requirements for justice and dignity. This applies to both internal and external communities as well as to organizational and interorganizational systems.

Because both individual rights and social justice are necessary conditions for a moral community, we can first examine individual rights and then decide what forms of justice they require, or we can first examine different forms of justice and see what rights individuals have in such communities. We just need to keep justice and rights together. When rights become separated from just forms of community, the basic tradition of rights as protests against injustice becomes distorted into a tradition of rights as a means for personal gain. The final purpose for individual rights is the development of a just community, just as the final purpose for justice is the development of a community that respects individual rights.

Since we are concerned with rights within organizations and want to give some guidelines for managing systems of power distribution, we will begin with an examination of justice and then turn to the question of employee and corporate rights. We need to ask once again the question that has always been the first question of social ethics: "What is justice?" Our answer will give us a base for engaging in open dialogue on many issues of employee and corporate rights that need answers today: rights to benefits, rights to receive and withhold information, rights to compensation for injury, rights to representation, rights to termination only for cause, rights to privacy, and so on.

Although justice is usually defined as treating equals equally and unequals unequally, one of the major tasks for a theory of justice is to justify treating people unequally. We need to know what conditions can justify treating people differently. Some may protest against equal treatment, such as when someone who contributes more than others on a project receives the same recognition as everyone else, but in most cases problems of justice come about because of unequal treatment.

Different treatment can be justified if it conforms to one of several standards of justice. In some instances, we all deserve equal treatment because of our basic humanity. In other instances, we usually agree to other forms of justice. If we are distributing medicine, for example, most people would distribute it according to need. If we are distributing scholarships, we distribute them according to merit. Actually, we commonly use one of several criteria for distributing resources, including *membership* (or equality — all members receive the same), *need* (those with greater need receive more), *contribution* (those who give more receive more), *merit* (according to status or talent), and *entitlement* (what individuals choose). We need to know when to use which criteria so that we correctly distinguish between justified and unjustified differences or inequalities. To give us some means for making such distinctions, we will briefly examine how some contemporary theories of justice handle inequalities, and then with this basis we will go on to discuss employee and corporate rights.

Contemporary Views of Justice

Theories of justice range from an extreme individualism — where each person gets to keep whatever he or she can get — to a total communalism — where everything should be equally distributed. Between these extremes, three contemporary options are Robert Nozick's libertarianism, John Rawls's social liberalism, and Michael Walzer's pluralistic justice.

The basis for the libertarian view of justice, according to Nozick, is that "individuals have rights" (1974, p. ix). If justice means anything, it means a social order that protects individual rights. Nozick believes these rights should be limited only by the equal rights of others or when the violation of others' rights has occurred and it is necessary for some kind of rectification of past wrongs (1974, p. 152). Emphasizing the right of individual choice, Nozick formulates the principle of justice as *"From each as they choose, to each as they are chosen"* (1974, p. 160). His view of justice is basically an entitlement theory: people should receive what they are entitled to through their own productivity, exchanges, and choices. The strength of the libertarian option is certainly its recognition of individual productivity. Some people do produce more and contribute more than others, and if they acquire more in the process — without infringing on the freedom of others — they are entitled to do what they want with their acquisitions. Denying this right seems to deny the meaning of the right to pursue one's own interest and life plan. The rights usually associated with the libertarian view include the rights to property, free association, voluntary exchanges, and free speech.

Assuming the equal right to choose one's work and to make fair exchanges at work for promotions and rewards, the libertarian could justify most inequalities in organizations. What the libertarian would not accept are patterns of distribution that override individual choice or fair exchanges. However, if persons freely choose to enter into subservient relationships, then the libertarian would not object to the resulting inequality. In the case of the temporary workers discussed in Chapter Seven, if employees freely chose to work on a temporary basis, then the libertarian would have no quarrel.

The weakness of this option, however, is that it seems to ignore the systemic character of modern society — the interdependence of systems components and the power of organizations. What organizational member can argue, "I did it all by myself"? We cannot talk on the phone or develop projects or complete assignments without depending on a vast network that gives and takes from everyone to the advantage of some and the disadvantage of others. If we take seriously a systems approach, which places the basic power of organizations in the organization itself rather than in any individual who has a particular role, then the libertarian option appears to have a rather narrow application. For those inequalities in organizations that arise from the system's design rather than from individual choice, a view of justice that speaks only of individual choice will not give us much help in justifying organizational inequalities.

What can be called the social liberal view of justice affirms the principle of equal liberty that the libertarian honors, but it adds to this a concern for a system's distribution of advantages and disadvantages. As John Rawls argues, "It is these inequalities, presumably inevitable in the basic structure of any society, to which the principles of social justice must in the first instance apply" (1971, p. 60). And what are these principles of social justice? Rawls argues for two, which he calls the principle of equal liberty and the principle of difference. The principle of equal liberty affirms that each person is free to do what he or she wants as long as this does not infringe on or interfere with another's liberty. Nozick and Rawls would have little disagreement about this first principle. The second principle — the difference principle — extends the social liberal option beyond the libertarian view. With it, Rawls attempts to show how inequalities — differences — can be justified. They can be justified, he argues, when the advantages of the "haves" work also to the advantage of the "have-nots." Furthermore, the positions of advantage, Rawls argues, must be open to all. Here is his formulation of the two principles: "First: each person is to have an equal right to the most extensive basic liberty compatible with a similar liberty for others. Second: social and economic inequalities are to be arranged so that they are both (a) reasonably expected to be to everyone's advantage, and (b) attached to positions and offices open to all" (1971, p. 60).

Do we agree with these two principles? Rawls seeks to

gain our consent in the following manner. He asks us to imagine ourselves in what he calls an "original position," which has two important characteristics. First of all, we do not know our exact position in society, whether we are well educated or not, employed or unemployed, and so on. We do know that such positions exist, but we do not know what place we occupy. Rawls calls this characteristic of the original position the "veil of ignorance" (1971, p. 136). The second characteristic is that we do have some general knowledge of what he calls the "circumstances of justice." This knowledge gives us reason to want to develop principles that will relate to such circumstances, which he describes as follows: "Thus, one can say, in brief, that the circumstances of justice obtain whenever mutually disinterested persons put forward conflicting claims to the division of social advantages under conditions of moderate scarcity. Unless these circumstances existed there would be no occasion for the virtue of justice, just as in the absence of threats of injury to life and limb there would be no occasion for physical courage" (1971, p. 128). So, we do not know what position we will have, but we do know that society will contain advantages and disadvantages and that people will seek what is to their advantage in regard to obtaining social and economic goods.

Given this hypothetical situation, what principles of justice would we consent to? Rawls thinks that rational people would agree to his principles: first, that everyone should have equal liberty; second, that any increase of advantage for those already in advantaged positions should also increase the advantage of others or, as he sometimes argues, the least advantaged; finally, that those positions of advantage should be open to everyone. If we would agree to these principles, then we could justify differences in the distribution of organizational resources, as long as these differences actually functioned to the benefit of even those members who did not receive them.

If we use Rawls's theory of justice, then the inequalities in organizations could be evaluated in terms of their effect on the least advantaged. This could probably justify differences in salary and promotions if they also benefited those not promoted. Such would be the case if those promoted actually increased the productivity of the organization in such a way that everyone benefited. This assumes that distributing more organizational power to some also empowers the rest. Rawls's theory of justice would also insist that these positions were open for all.

In terms of rights, Rawls's first principle of justice essentially affirms the rights that Nozick also affirms — the rights of equal liberty. Rawls's second principle of justice, the difference principle, does seem to justify a right to something like one's "fair share" (Fried, 1978, p. 110). For any advantage that others receive, the least advantaged have a right not to an equal share but to their fair share. However, for the social liberal this right to a fair share would not allow the curtailment of the basic rights of liberty. But what is a fair share? The notion of a fair share differs from the rights of liberty because it would require some pattern of distribution to ensure that the shares were distributed fairly. Organizational systems, of course, are already patterns of distribution. The question is whether all members receive their fair share of what is distributed. For promotions, a fair share may be equal consideration for the job. It certainly cannot mean that everyone receives a promotion. A fair share is not necessarily an equal share. Some may receive more and some less, but they would see the division as fair. To determine whether a pattern of distribution is fair, we can return to the original position where we do not know who will receive what share and develop a pattern of distribution that we can agree with. Since we do not know whether we will receive more or less, we will develop a system that may be unequal but will be fair. This may include promotions based on past contributions or leadership ability. As long as everyone has a fair chance to . make such contributions and to learn leadership skills, then we might agree that everyone received a fair share of the resources within the system.

Turning again to the case of the temporary worker, Rawls's view of justice allows us to ask two different questions. First of all, we can use Rawls's notion of the original position and ask if we would agree to such a job structure. Since we would not know our own place but assume the general condition of employers and employees, would we agree that organizations could have largely temporary workers, knowing that we might become one? We can also apply Rawls's second principle of justice and ask if the advantages of this system of justice would also be advantageous for the disadvantaged. Temporary positions could benefit those who like working without any responsibility for the organization as well as some managers. But do these advantages also work to the advantage of the most disadvantaged — perhaps those who must work and yet cannot ask for equity because of fear they will be replaced by "cheaper" temporary workers? Rawls's second principle of justice would prompt us to design organizations so that the unequal distribution of power would benefit not only those in positions of power but also those in positions of less power.

Another way of justifying differences in distribution is to look at the meaning and function of the distributed goods. Michael Walzer's *Spheres of Justice: A Defense of Pluralism and Equality* (1983) offers us such a strategy. He takes into account much more of the actual character of our different institutions than does either Nozick or Rawls. Even more important, he takes seriously our experience that many different kinds of things are distributed differently: "that the principles of justice are themselves pluralistic in form; that different social goods ought to be distributed for different reasons, in accordance with different procedures, by different agents; and that all these differences derive from different understandings of the social goods themselves — the inevitable product of historical and cultural particularism" (1983, p. 6).

What is justice? Well, it depends. It depends on our cultural and social development, on the meanings attributed to things, and on the particular sphere in which they are distributed. Instead of limiting justice to a simple equality that seeks a universal standard, Walzer extends justice to a complex equality that takes into account the differences between different goods. These goods find their meaning in the social construction of reality — that is, in our way of attributing meaning to things in our continuing and changing culture. The goods are such things as security and welfare, money, office, recognition, education, kinship and love, and power. Each of these, Walzer maintains, has its own criteria for distribution. When they are distributed according to their own criteria, the distribution is just; when distributed by other criteria, unjust. Unjust distribution actually signals tyranny, because outside criteria are used to dominate a sphere where they have no place.

Money, for example, belongs to the exchange of commodities and so has a place in the market system. However, when money is used to buy votes (the political sphere) or grace (the religious sphere), its use is unjust. Since we live in a society where it sometimes seems that money can buy everything, Walzer's list of what money cannot buy aptly demonstrates the need for a variety of criteria. Money cannot buy human beings; political power; criminal justice; freedom of speech, press, religion, and assembly; marriage and procreation rights; the right to leave the political community; exemption from military service; political offices; basic welfare services such as police protection; desperate exchanges; trades of last resort; prizes and honors; divine grace; love and friendship; and criminal acts (Walzer, 1983, pp. 100–103). All of these belong to spheres other than that of money. To use money to acquire them is unjust. At the same time, to use other criteria such as race or religion to exclude some from the market is unjust since, in this sphere, whoever has money has the right to engage in the market system.

Another sphere where money should not reign is what Walzer calls the sphere of office (1983, p. 164). *Office* here refers to a career and includes administrative offices, corporate offices, and professional service offices. These offices are not commodities, sold to the highest bidder, but rather go to those qualified— those who have the qualifications for the particular office. To distribute offices by other criteria such as family ties or wealth or power is unjust.

As we already know, power is distributed in organizational systems, but Walzer also gives us a method for determining how it should be distributed. For productive organizations, Walzer suggests, there comes a point when power passes out of the control of those who founded the organization and must be reorganized in some other way. Walzer's suggestion agrees with Galbraith's notion of organizational power as different from personal or property power, which was discussed in the last chapter. When an organization itself becomes the basis for its power, then neither personality nor property should function as a criterion for distribution. Instead, Walzer argues, the system of distribution should be determined "according to the prevailing (democratic) conception of how power ought to be distributed" (1983, p. 303). In other words, the just way of distributing power will depend on the members' understanding of the meaning of the resources, roles, and relations that constitute organizational power, or, in Walzer's terms, "Justice is relative to social meanings" (1983, p. 312). What resources mean, in other words, depends on a community's experiences of and conversations about organizational life.

If we apply Walzer's view of justice to the temporary workers case, then we need to discuss the social meaning of work. If part of the social meaning of work is membership in a moral community and if participation in such a community gives people meaning as well as contributes to the community itself, then the practice of temporary work would seem to radically change the meaning of work. Meanings do change, of course, as changes in the related notion of job security illustrate. Not so long ago, security was distributed to those who stayed with and were loyal to the company. Partly as a result of the labor struggle for seniority, security not only for workers but also for managers was something that workers "deserved." In the past decade, the distribution of jobs and promotions has changed dramatically. Sometimes jobs and promotions are used as a reward for high performance or even as a motivation for performance. In a strange way, job security now depends on insecurity — only by continuing to reach performance goals can one have "secure" employment. In terms of Boulding's three maintenance factors, this shift in the meaning of work has increased the subsystems of threat and exchange and decreased the subsystem of integration. Another effect has been a more individualistic work force, with many workers committed not to the corporation but to their own career development. Instead of security, individuals seek competence so that they can continue to find work even in periods of rapid change. The meaning of work today therefore involves a greater emphasis on continual learning and acquiring new skills than in previous decades. These make up some of the goods that workplaces distribute, and corporations must decide what criteria to use in distributing them. Whether these changes increase or decrease the meaning of work is another question, which Chapter Nine will address when different assumptions about the work force are examined. These changes in meaning have also raised new questions about the rights of employees and corporations.

Walzer's notion of complex equality places rights within the context of the different spheres of justice. From this perspective, justice is the foundation for rights. If justice serves as the foundation for rights, then rights would be derived from membership in different communities. Rights, in other words, depend on the social meanings of the different goods to which one has a right. Walzer recognizes the right of liberty and the right to equal consideration, but the justification for these different rights is "less of a Universalist conception of persons than a pluralist conception of goods" (1983, p. xv). What actual rights persons have, in other words, depends on the social meaning of the goods available to the community and the social meaning of the community itself.

To speak of rights, we need to first determine the social meaning of things, but things have different meanings for different people. The social meaning of basic provisions, for example, may differ for the rich and the poor. Only by including both groups in the conversation will the community know the meaning of basic provisions. When some groups are denied participation in such debates, those who deny them practice a form of tyranny by overriding their basic right to be active members of a community and to participate in the determination of the meaning of things (Walzer, 1983, p. 83). For Walzer, rights, like justice, will be decided through the continuing conversation among members of the different communities about the social meanings of communal goods. The one right that such conversations assume is the right of participation, the right to a voice in the decision-making process: "The citizen must be ready and able, when his time comes, to deliberate with his fellows, listen and be listened to, take responsibility for what he says and does. Ready and able: not only in states, cities, and towns, but wherever power is exercised in companies and factories, too, and in unions, faculties, and professions. Deprived permanently of power, whether at national or local levels, he is deprived also of this sense of himself. Hence the reversal of Lord Acton's maxim, attributed to a variety of twentieth-century politicans and writers: 'Power corrupts, but the lack of power corrupts absolutely'" (1983, p. 310).

To provide a comprehensive view of justice and rights, we can incorporate the strengths of all three theories we have discussed. Nozick's theory of entitlement highlights the rights of individuals to their own power, which no one without justification can limit. Entitlements would include the equal rights of liberty. At the same time, a systems perspective would insist that any adequate understanding of how we live together not ignore the multitude of interconnections and mutual dependencies of our organizational life. We also need Rawls's principle of difference, which recognizes mutual dependence and draws from it the notion of mutual advantage. By analyzing the historical development of the meaning of goods and basing justice on such meanings, Walzer provides a contextual analysis of rights that seems particularly applicable to organizations. Rights become a reflection of our systems of justice, which are based on the meaning of the goods for the community in which they are distributed.

When we seek to justify inequalities, Nozick asks us how the inequalities came about. If they are the result of free choices and did not infringe on the equal freedom of others, then they could be justified. Rawls asks us to think about whether we could accept how such inequalities came about if we were in an "original position." Could we imagine ourselves in any of the unequal positions? And Walzer asks us if the inequalities in distribution matched our notion of the meaning of the goods distributed. If so, they could be justified; if not, the inequality represents a kind of tyranny where inappropriate criteria were used for distributing communal goods. As a way of discerning what different goods means, we can examine the list of organizational goods in Exhibit 1 and decide how they should be distributed by the five criteria of membership, need, contribution, merit, and entitlement.

Exhibit 1.

To ascertain your own notion of justice in organizations, select one of the five criteria for distribution for each of the goods listed.

Goods		Criteria for Distribution
Safety	____	1. Contribution (those who give more receive more)
Bonuses	____	
Benefits	____	2. Need (those who need more receive more)
Leisure	____	
Information	____	3. Membership (distributed equally to all members)
Recognition	____	
Job security	____	4. Merit (distributed according to status or talent)
Compensation	____	
Due process	____	5. Entitlement (acquired by people on their own)
Advancement	____	
Privacy	____	

The kinds of justice you think should be used to distribute the goods listed in Exhibit 1 will give you some idea of what they mean to you and your organization. To find their more complete social meaning, you could imagine how others think they should be distributed, and why. This will offer a fuller understanding of what justice means to your organization and to social communities beyond your organization.

You can also determine what rights follow from the types of justice you have selected. For example, if safety should be distributed according to membership (equally to all members), then on the other side of that system of justice we can assert the right to such safety. Or, if we said that bonuses should be distributed according to contribution, then those who contribute have a right to such a bonus. However, if bonuses were distributed according to need, then those who contributed more would not have such a right. Inequalities in power and in resources that correspond to our understanding of justice and rights could be justified. Those inequalities that do not correspond should be changed. The worksheet on rights and justice in Chapter Eleven (Exhibit 7) provides an opportunity for individuals and groups to analyze what goods their organization distributes and under what types of justice and with respect to what kinds of rights.

As stated earlier, we can learn about our rights by studying justice, or we can learn about just organizations by studying rights. Determining what rights individuals have can tell us what constitutes a just distribution of resources and power. A right to information that affects one's safety, for example, requires that information about safety be distributed according to membership or the need to know. The assertion of rights usually occurs in unjust situations, where resources and power have been unfairly distributed. Much of the tradition of human rights, in fact, has involved protests against the abuse of power and against unjustifiable inequalities. As the discussion turns to the topic of employee and corporate rights, you can see how it conforms to what we have already learned about justice.

Employee Rights

Employee rights (which includes management) are derived from the different communities in which employees live. These communities include the human community, a national community, and the corporate community where they work. To understand all the rights that employees are entitled to, we need to understand something about these different communities and their relationships to one another. As members of organizations, we have contractual and institutional rights. As members of nations, we have civil and legal rights. And as members of the human family, or the global community, we have moral and human rights.

We can image these different communities and the rights they entail as concentric circles. All three circles involve both human communities and systems of maintenance and productivity, both of which must be taken into account to fully understand the responsibilities their rights entail. Understanding each system's resources will allow us to see what claims for rights are legitimate claims on power or legitimate protests against injustice or the abuse of power. Furthermore, the circle of employee and corporate rights is embedded in the circle of legal rights, and these rights are embedded in the wider circle of human rights. If we begin with the outer circle and move toward the inner circle, then we begin with our membership in the global community, where all members have human rights.

The modern notion of human rights rests on "our ideas of what it is to be human" (Minogue, 1979, p. 14). These ideas have usually been formulated along with some form of community, as in the 1948 United Nations Declaration of Human Rights, which states: "Everyone, as a member of society, has the right to social security and is entitled to realization, through national effort and international co-operation and in accordance with the organization and resources of each State, of the economic, social, and cultural rights indispensable for his dignity and the free development of his personality" (Laqueur and Rubin, 1979, p. 200). Every person—which means every employee of a corporation—belongs to this community, and ultimately their membership here serves as the basis for these rights. At the same time, what happens in the global community ultimately affects the rights of everyone. A systems perspective, which assumes the interrelatedness of all its parts, would encourage all employees to see that their destiny is intertwined with the destiny of the whole system, as many American workers have experienced in the past decades as their jobs were exported to other countries. As a member of society or a member of the human family, employees have human rights, and especially applicable to their status as employees is article 23 of the United Nations Declaration:

1. Everyone has a right to work, to free choice of employment, to just and favorable conditions of work, and to protection against unemployment.
2. Everyone, without any discrimination, has a right to equal pay for equal work.
3. Everyone who works has the right to just and favorable remuneration insuring for himself and his family an existence worthy of human

dignity, and supplemented, if necessary, by
other means of social protection.
4.   Everyone has the right to form and to join trade
unions for the protection of his interests [La-
queur and Rubin, 1979, p. 200].

Since rights can only be completely understood in light of
the communities in which they make sense and the systems that
distribute the resources to which rights refer, an understanding
of the real meaning of these rights requires us to analyze the global
systems and their current relationship with the global community. If we use Boulding's system organizers of threat, exchange,
and integration, even a cursory examination certainly reveals
a global system suffering from excessive threats, unequal exchanges, and a lack of integration. American foreign aid illustrates this imbalance fairly well. In 1985, for example, American foreign aid was distributed as follows: military assistance,
62 percent; food, 10 percent; development assistance, 25 percent; and other, 3 percent. These figures do not include any covert
aid (Folbre, 1987). Although we cannot carry out a satisfactory
analysis here, we can cite examples of the employment of the
threat, exchange, and integration organizers. There are countless
instances, from Latin America to South Africa, where threats — if
not military intervention — have been used. The Western banks
forcing Third World governments to decrease their social programs as a condition for refinancing their loans shows some of
the effects of using exchange organizers at the expense of integration. They ensured not only their own wealth but also an increase
in poverty. Changes in the exchange organizer have also brought
about greater equality, as when the Arab oil boycott resulted in
a fairer exchange between those nations that supply resources
and those nations that use those resources. There are also examples of systems changes through increasing integration, such as
the dramatic "fall" of the Berlin Wall in 1989 and the movements
toward a united economic Europe. We certainly know that the
global systems will continue to change, and which organizer drives
the change will determine the degree of justice and the actual rights
members of the global community will enjoy.

Within the context of human rights, employees in the

United States as well as other nations also can claim certain civil and legal rights — the second foundation for employee rights. Through the bitter labor struggles of the late nineteenth and early twentieth centuries as well as through the growth of progressive political power, American workers translated many of their human rights into legal rights. This process, of course, continues, as we witness in debates over such issues as employment at will. It is interesting that the United States is virtually the only Western country that does not protect employees against unjust discharge (Hall, 1987, p. 164). This situation may change, just as legal rights are changing in other areas. For example, even though the term *privacy* is not mentioned in the Constitution, recent cases have led the courts to see it as consistent with what the Constitution's authors intended. In 1965, in the *Griswold* v. *Connecticut* decision, the Supreme Court recognized a person's right to "a 'zone of privacy' around their person that could not be violated by the government" (Des Jardins, 1987, p. 128). We can assume that our legal rights will continue to change as we gain more awareness of the fuller consequences of human or universal rights for the communities in which we all live.

Some employee rights have their basis not so much in human or legal rights as in employment agreements and in job descriptions or organizational roles. Parties of a contract have a right to see the terms of the contract fulfilled as long as the contract itself is valid. Contractual rights have their basis in the validity of the contract itself. The following four points must be fulfilled for a contract to be valid: (1) Both parties have full knowledge of the agreement. (2) Neither party intentionally misrepresents the facts to the other. (3) Neither party is forced to enter the contract under duress or coercion. (4) The contract must not bind the parties to immoral acts (Velasquez, 1988, pp. 89–90). The employment contract, however, differs somewhat from a contract to purchase a commodity because "what is bought and sold is not a definite objective thing, but rather a personal relation" (Arrow, 1974, p. 64). The kind of personal relation, of course, depends on the contract, but at least in many settings it is a relationship of authority, an agreement to work for someone and to follow his or her instructions. Do employees lose any of their human or legal rights when they begin to work for an organization?

If we take the right to liberty in its laissez-faire sense —
that is, as "leave me alone" — then the work contract does limit
one's liberty. Entering voluntarily into the employee contract
requires employees to fulfill the contractual terms and to work
for the corporation rather than for themselves. Such contracts,
however, cannot involve the relinquishing of human or civil
rights, because that would make the contract itself dehumaniz-
ing and therefore invalid. If contracts cannot bind the parties
to immoral acts, then they cannot entail the limiting of human
or civil rights. In fact, these rights provide the ultimate basis
for contracts. Without the power and responsibility — that is,
the moral agency — of the parties, the contract becomes either
merely a piece of paper or a form of tyranny. Employees as persons, as members of society, and as members of organizations
have different kinds of rights. Ultimately, they parallel the different kinds of justice that we develop in our different communities. Do corporations have the same rights?

Corporate Rights

Corporations also exist within the global community of
human rights, and their first responsibility as part of the global
system is to practice, within their power, the justice the system
requires to ensure these rights. As subsystems within the larger
system, corporations can either promote system vitality or mis-
appropriate the system's resources for themselves. We could employ Rawls's principle of difference to evaluate corporate action,
which would lead us to see if those policies that enhanced the
corporation also enhanced the disadvantaged. Since international
corporations largely control the resources of the global system,
and since the global system itself lacks an adequate legal basis
for preventing the abuse of this power, corporations have a
responsibility to consider their actions themselves and to listen
to those who give a voice to the injustices of the current global
system. Furthermore, since the actual distribution of global
resources certainly determines the possibilities of actually respecting human rights, productive and responsive corporations do
have the responsibility for respecting human rights.

Corporations in the United States also have rights. These include a variety of legal rights. Their legal status as "persons" gives them many of the same rights as other citizens. As members of the republic, they enjoy such rights as protection against unreasonable searches or seizures — the Fourth Amendment — and the right of due process and equal protection — the Fourteenth Amendment (Davidson and others, 1987, p. 839). Corporations have the civil rights that belong to any citizen of the nation in which they are incorporated. They also have rights accorded to them in their articles of incorporation, for example, the rights to conduct business, to exist perpetually, and to make a profit. The common-law tradition of defining the duties and rights of the master-servant relationship gives corporations a set of rights called the "law of agency." It defines the rights and obligations of the employer-employee relationship. The employer, or "principle," essentially has the right to tell the employee, or "agent," what to do and how to do it (Davidson and others, 1987, p. 706).

Corporations also have the right to expect employees not to harm the corporation or to work against its interests. The law of agency, however, rests on a master-servant relationship, which does not seem to recognize the full moral rights of humans. *Servants* is not a term that assumes equal freedom. Today, however, citizens do enjoy such rights, and in many cases the corporation cannot require that the citizen-employee relinquish them.

Corporations also enjoy the rights given in the contracts they make. Employment contracts, for example, usually give corporations the right to expect specific performances from employees. These contracts actually give rights and duties to both the corporation and the employee.

In discussing the rights of corporations, we need to make a distinction between legal and human or moral rights. Although the two may coincide, they may also differ. Changes in our laws, such as the laws regarding slavery and later segregation, illustrate the continuing story of how our moral rights not only differ from but also change our legal rights. The law of agency faces a similar historical pressure because it is founded on an archaic notion of master-servant relationship that no longer corresponds with current thinking about employee-employer relationships. Corporations continually experience such changes as governments enact laws to protect our air, water, land, and wildlife as well as our social environment. It is possible that the continuing moral development of our society may eventually change the current legal rights of corporations.

Do corporations have human rights as well as legal rights? In other words, do the rights of corporations as artificial persons differ from the rights of human beings as flesh-and-blood persons? The philosopher Immanuel Kant's distinction between what has dignity and what has a price can help us answer that question ([1785] 1964b, p. 102). He reasoned that humans have a dignity that cannot be bought or sold. Although he did not talk about corporations, they certainly are bought and sold. They have their price. You can buy "the whole thing." But should you be able to? Is a corporation only a commodity? If we interpret corporations as complex systems of productivity and maintenance as well as moral communities, then treating them as merely things seems inappropriate. As Galbraith has argued, the primary power of organizations is not property but rather organization. A human organization certainly has value, even human value, and treating it only as a piece of property misses this completely. The buying and selling of corporations as though they were merely property would be a kind of tyranny, which unjustly uses a criterion for distribution — money — in a sphere in which it does not belong. The fact that corporations can be traded does not tell us how we ought to treat them, only how we presently do treat them. To determine how they should be treated requires us to uncover their social meaning, which is embedded in their moral communities and systems of maintenance and productivity. Corporate rights, based on this social meaning of corporations, should be respected but should also remain limited. Corporations still do not have the same rights as humans, and if human rights are fundamental, at least in the sense that the human community has priority over the corporate system, then corporate rights should not override human rights. From this position, we can describe a corporation's rights by examining the law *and* by looking at how its policies and practices affect the legal and moral rights of flesh-and-blood persons — whether it respects human dignity. Here we assume a traditional principle of rights — namely, that persons can exercise their rights to the extent that they do not violate the rights of others.

With these distinctions between different kinds of rights, we can ask if corporations have such rights as the right to spy on workers, to send in undercover observers to see if workers are working as they should, and to use cameras to monitor the workshop. First of all, does this monitoring violate the rights of workers? Corporate rights end where human rights extend. Second, if this is a violation of rights, is it illegal or immoral or both? Secret monitoring could violate the principle of human dignity if it treats employees as things rather than as persons, if it discounts their integrity, and if it erodes mutual trust. If spying has these effects, then it not only violates individual dignity but also erodes the basis of organizational life.

Remember former Secretary of State George Shultz's response to a somewhat parallel case involving trust? When he was asked to take a lie-detector test, he refused because he felt that if he was not trusted, he should resign. He set a limit of a corporation's right to use its power. He also implicitly recognized that trust and not threat is the only sure foundation for organizational effectiveness. Systems of threat cannot build or even maintain organizational community. At the very most, they can only preserve it. When systems of threat override human rights, however, they then fail to perform even this function. Human rights as a protest against the abuse of power and as a demand for justice can preserve community. But the community itself requires the practice of justice to sustain itself — a pluralistic justice that distributes the community's different goods according to their meaning for human life.

Debates about such issues as drug testing, honesty tests, and monitoring depend on our notions of justice and rights and how these standards protect the power of employees and legitimate corporate power. Rights may restrain power when the unequal distribution of power prevents some from exercising their basic humanity. Justice can guide the distribution of power according to the meaning of resources for the total community. Together, rights and justice can set standards for the maintenance of a powerful, responsible organization. What standards of justice we use in guiding organizations and their relations to larger communities, as Walzer has suggested, depend on the social meaning of our resources. In groups comprised of different organizational constituencies, or even from different organizational levels or divisions, participants will probably give different meanings to our resources. Part of the process of dealing with claims for rights and justice is to discover and resolve the disagreements about the meaning of organizational life. This type of disagreement will largely rest on different values and assumptions about the self, others, and the functioning of organizational life. Addressing these issues will probably begin with an analysis of basic assumptions, which is discussed in the next chapter.

Chapter Nine

Resolving Differences Between Assumptions and Values

Although we always interpret data and make observations from our basic assumptions, and they certainly influence what we focus on and how we tend to interpret experiences, our assumptions also have significant relationships with our value judgments and important implications for the whole process of decision making (O'Toole, 1985; Mason and Mitroff, 1981). On the one hand, the presence of persons with different assumptions may explain a group's inability to agree on a policy when they agree on the data and value judgments. On the other hand, if a group shares similar assumptions, it can find ways to deal with its disagreements about what value judgments should have priority. Also, when a group examines the organizational system and evaluates it in terms of justice and individual rights, participants' assumptions may lead them to select different types of justice or emphasize different rights as criteria for evaluating the system. Disagreements about how to manage the balance of threat, exchange, and integration patterns to maintain an organization can also be traced to different assumptions. To get ethics to work, then, we need some strategies for analyzing assumptions.

Sometimes we use the term assumption to refer to our expectations, as in statements like "Oh, I assumed he did not care about what happened." Researchers may also assume, for example, that 30 percent of the respondents will answer their questionnaires in a particular way. In such cases, the assumption is a hypothesis or guess about what will happen. The term is used in a different sense here: Assumptions are our taken-for-granted understandings of the dynamics of individual and collective life. Our assumptions serve as the background for our interpretations of persons, of ourselves, and of social reality.

I use the term much like Edgar Schein does in his *Organizational Culture and Leadership,* where he defines an organization's culture as those *"basic assumptions* and *beliefs* that are shared by members of an organization, that operate unconsciously, and that define in a basic 'taken-for-granted' fashion an organization's view of itself and its environment" (italics his) (1985, p. 6).

Some may believe that assumptions actually are individual rather than cultural, but once they begin to encounter other cultures, it usually becomes clear that the notion of individual assumptions itself belongs to a particular cultural history. Assumptions of individual autonomy and independence belong to Western cultures, and even within that culture, some subcultures hold those assumptions more strongly than others. Whenever we analyze our own assumptions, we are also understanding our cultural background.

Culture includes more than national or ethnic identity. Especially in the West, our cultural background and the basis for our assumptions originates first of all in our family life and later in our experiences and learning in institutions and society. Organizations, too, as Schein has demonstrated, have a culture, which he defines as "a pattern of basic assumptions — invented, discovered, or developed by a given group as it learns to cope with its problems of external adaptation and internal integration — that has worked well enough to be considered valid and, therefore, to be taught to new members as the correct way to perceive, think, and feel in relation to those problems" (1985, p. 9).

Although we want to affirm the notion of a corporate culture, most organizations are probably not as homogeneous as one might think but rather have individuals and groups who interpret events with different assumptions, primarily because they come from different family and social cultures. Since we have focused on a strategy for ethical reflection when people disagree about what should be done, our analysis naturally focuses on the dynamics of differences and similarities among the parts of an organization rather than the assumptions of the whole. When all parts of an organization share the same assumptions, and as long as these assumptions allow the organization to interact creatively with its environment, then assumptions will probably keep their taken-for-granted status. With the rapid change of organizations and the environment, however, most organizations cannot avoid disagreement for very long. Instead of assuming that everyone in an organization shares the same assumptions, we recognize the possibility of different assumptions among individuals, organizations, and an organization's different constituencies. Especially in changing organizations, we may encounter conflicting assumptions much more often than similar ones.

Some writers, such as Deal and Kennedy, have used the category of values to refer to the basis of a corporation's culture (1982, p. 24). The distinction between values and assumptions, however, allows us to consider both what one values and how one assumes it can be obtained. We can see the advantages of this distinction by looking at two different cases: one case where people share similar values but have different assumptions, and another case where people affirm different values, but share the same assumptions.

For the first case, let us say Mike and George both value security and decide to build a new house. Mike assumes that people basically live for themselves and will take advantage of others if they have a chance. For him, the world is a jungle. George, in contrast, assumes that people desire community and closeness and that they take care of each other in times of need. As you might suspect, they build very different kinds of houses. Mike builds on a lot separated from other houses. His house has few windows; it looks like a fortress. George builds his house close to other houses; and throughout the house one notices openness to the neighborhood. Both builders had security in mind when they built their homes, but they became secure very differently because they had different assumptions about the world.

The second case involves two team workers: Juanita and Maureen. Juanita wants to further her education and develop a different career in another field. So she sees her present job as a means to acquire the financial base to eventually realize her goals. Maureen wants to become a corporate manager and sees her present job as a means for future promotions. Juanita's and Maureen's different values could disrupt their teamwork but may not if they share some basic assumptions. If they have similar pragmatic attitudes or basic assumptions about individual choice or about tolerance for differences as well as similar assumptions about putting in a day's work, then they can probably find a common ground to work together. Their different values, in other words, can fit into a larger context of shared assumptions. By making the distinction between values and assumptions, we can develop strategies to find agreements when at first glance it looks unlikely.

Another aspect of assumptions that sometimes distinguishes them from values is that assumptions are cultural. Some values are cultural, too, but many are social. Therefore, people who belong to different social groups or classes may have different values, and yet if they belong to the same culture, share similar cultural assumptions. Members of organizations, for example, tend to take on the values of their departments such as the values of marketing, finance, human resources, and senior management. All these social groups in an organization, however, may share the same cultural assumptions. Each of these groups may emphasize its own department's values and yet share the assumption that "things eventually even out."

To discover the connections between values and assumptions, one needs to begin analyzing the assumptions that seem pertinent in the actual process of making decisions or in evaluating organizational systems. Before we can begin to examine our assumptions, however, we have to become aware of them. Actually, analyzing assumptions requires two different steps: first becoming aware of them and then evaluating them.

Becoming Aware of Assumptions

Because assumptions are taken for granted, and even unconscious, their analysis usually requires some event to bring them to our attention. When all members share the same assumptions, then the normal process of developing policy will probably not call them to mind. When people do not share the same assumptions or when their assumptions no longer "fit" their experiences, assumptions become easier to grasp. An employee may automatically assume, for example, that a manager will appreciate a suggestion on how to improve his or her relationship with a co-worker. The employee may make the suggestion without thinking and then discover that the manager spurns the suggestion and the co-worker resents the interference. Such experiences usually make our assumptions painfully clear. Although assumptions are made conscious by such surprises, in many decision-making processes we do not have the luxury of making mistakes. The following are some different ways we can become aware of assumptions.

Investigating Differences. We have all experienced changes in our assumptions. Most of us can fill in the following blanks without much difficulty: I once assumed_____, but now I assume_____. Experiences of changed assumptions give us clues about how we become aware of them. They usually seem to fall into one of two patterns. Either our old assumptions no longer work, or we encounter other assumptions that seem more appropriate for ourselves or our organization.

Sometimes, we listen to what others have observed about ourselves or our culture, and that alone changes our assumptions. For example, Carol Gilligan (1982) showed us that men and women tend to use different frameworks when interpreting ethical dilemmas. In her study of eleven-year-old boys and girls, she found that the girls interpreted an ethical dilemma differently than the boys did. The dilemma involved a simple case of a man considering whether to steal a drug that he could not afford in order to save his wife. The boys tended to interpret the situation as a conflict of principle and thought that the principle of saving a life should override the principle of not stealing. The girls, in contrast, tried to think of other ways to get the drug such as borrowing the necessary money and paying it back later. Gilligan interprets these different responses as a difference between the boys' use of abstract principles — they saw the issue as one of formal justice — and the girls' attempt to find a solution — they saw the problem as a "failure of response" (1982, p. 28). Gilligan continues in her book to develop a "feminist ethic" that she terms an *ethic of care* as opposed to an ethic of principle. Her ethic of care resembles an ethic of consequence, where one cares for what happens to those involved rather than focusing on ideas. These different ethical theories, some of which we discussed in Chapter Five, may lead us to think about our own assumptions and bring to our attention what we have previously taken for granted.

Including Different Voices. We can also bring attention to assumptions by bringing together people from different subcultures. All of us belong to some subculture, even though some people live as though they belonged to a dominant culture and only others belonged to subcultures, but then that is another cultural assumption. If we want to become aware of our own assumptions, we can listen to and interact with groups or group representatives whose assumptions differ from ours. As our world becomes more interrelated, we need to ask more about how people arrive at their answers and to understand their process of evaluating situations.

Taking On Another's Assumptions. You can also discover assumptions by asking of positions you disagree with: "What would I have to assume to agree with that position?" For example, in the case of what to do after a mistake, discussed in Chapter Five, what would you have to assume to agree with those staff members who felt that Ralph should not be told about his cardiac arrest due to the medication overdose? You might have to believe that Ralph would not stay away from drugs unless he feared that using drugs might kill him. Supporting this belief might be the assumption that fear will work as a tool for compliance. Finally, you might assume that some people live their lives out of fear and, furthermore, that such living should — at least in this case — be promoted. You might carry this analysis further to see if the "pedagogy of fear" would extend to dealing with children or with others, or if you assume fear guides your own actions. Is fear a healthy motivator for human conduct? Posing such questions allows us to understand our own assumptions as well as to begin to think about them.

Developing Options. Because we live in a pluralistic culture where we encounter different assumptions, we can also discover assumptions by developing contrasting alternatives. For example, we can contrast the assumption that managers know more about how to organize the work force than workers with the alternative that workers know more than managers. By placing these alternatives at ends of a continuum, we can then see where our own assumptions might fall, depending on the specifics of what kind of knowledge we are considering.

Not all assumptions, of course, require analysis for reaching a decision, so participants in ethical reflection can use the policy question and the first steps of ethical reflection — the analysis of information and value judgments — as guides for selecting the assumptions that need analysis. Without these guidelines, the analysis of assumptions can lose its relevance. The two types of situations particularly important for ethical analysis in organizations are those (1) where participants share the same values and still cannot agree on what should be done and (2) where participants hold different values but may have similar assumptions.

Shared Values and Different Assumptions

The analysis of assumptions in the cases of shared values but different assumptions involves four steps: (1) state the specific value agreement, (2) develop opposing assumptions that seem relevant for applying the value, (3) draw a line with these opposing assumptions at opposite ends, and (4) have participants choose the place on the line that corresponds with their assumptions. We will use this strategy for five statements where people agree on values but disagree on assumptions. The first one concerns assumptions about finding out the truth:

> We may agree to do the right thing but have different assumptions about how to discover what it is.

The difference in assumptions here refers to how we discover the right action, a basic assumption for ethical reflection. To

develop some of the assumptions that people might have about
how to discover the right thing to do, we can use Schein's "topology of authority," which lists the following six assumptions
about how truth emerges:

1. Pure dogma, based on tradition and/or religion
2. Revealed dogma — that is, wisdom based on
    trust in the authority of wise men, formal
    leaders, prophets, or kings
3. Truth derived by a "rational-legal" process, as
    when we establish the guilt or innocence of an
    individual by means of a legal process that ac-
    knowledges from the outset that there is no ab-
    solute truth, only socially determined truth
4. Truth as that which survives conflict and de-
    bate
5. Truth as that which works, the purely prag-
    matic criterion
6. Truth as established by the scientific method,
    which becomes, once again, a kind of dogma
    [1985, p. 92].

Different organizations, of course, have different traditions of
finding and presenting the "truth." The Catholic church differs
from a New England town meeting, and a scientific laboratory
differs from a television talk show. The extremes of dialogue
and dogma seem the most relevant choices for most organizational settings. Dialogue would entail an open discussion where
everyone has a voice, and dogma would involve the use of experts or other authorities whose status makes them the voices
of truth. We will use these two terms as the opposing alternatives and place them at opposite ends of a line, which gives us
the following continuum:

Dialogue •   •   •   •   •   •   •   •   Dogma

Where people fit on this continuum, of course, partly depends on the group's task and resources. Most of us would po-

sition ourselves differently on the line if we were considering
a medical decision about surgery than if we were considering
a decision about a volunteer cleanup program. The first step
in analyzing the results, however, is not to see if participants
agree with our assumptions but rather to see if the group itself
holds similar or disparate assumptions. If the group participants
distribute themselves all over this continuum, then their different assumptions may be preventing them from making any
progress. Those who want the experts to say what should happen will not get a hearing from those who advocate an open
discussion about what to do, and vice versa. On the other hand,
bringing into consciousness the participants' different assumptions may give them a chance to clarify the group's tasks and
resources and to argue about which assumptions are most appropriate for this time and place.

The evaluation of assumptions, once they are uncovered,
can proceed by the asking of questions. Although some questions will pertain to specific cases, others have more general ap-
plicability. Four such general questions are (1) Which assumptions seem most relevant to the case? (2) Which assumptions
correspond to the group's assigned task and resources? (3) Which
assumptions are most consistent with other assumptions the
group has been working on? (4) Do some assumptions belong
more to other situations than to this one? Since most of us belong to or have belonged to different kinds of groups, with different task and resources, we can usually think of groups where
our assumptions would be most appropriate and where they
would be very inappropriate — for example, the difference between a medical consultation and a volunteer meeting. By imag-
ining appropriate and inappropriate places for specific assumptions, we can begin to understand how appropriate they are for
the current group. Whenever we evaluate assumptions, we can
ask the preceding questions as well as others that will arise out
of a group's particular purpose.

Because assumptions serve as the basis for our interpretation of things it is difficult to find someplace from which to
interpret them. The above questions, however, may serve as
a beginning for such an evaluation. The evaluation process de-

pends on the ability of the group to allow and at the same time to question differences. Whether that happens finally depends on the assumptions that the group has of itself and its members. We can look at alternative assumptions about that next, but in connection with the value of high productivity.

> We may value high productivity but hold different
> assumptions about how to achieve it.

How to achieve high productivity has been a major topic of management theory, and probably the most famous and useful theory has been McGregor's distinction between Theory X and Theory Y (1960, pp. 33–57). A Theory X view of the work force includes the following three propositions:

1. The average human being has an inherent dislike of work and will avoid it if he can.
2. Because of this characteristic human dislike of work, most people must be coerced, controlled, directed, and threatened with punishment to get them to put forth adequate effort toward the achievement of organizational objectives.
3. The average human being prefers to be directed, wishes to avoid responsibility, has relatively little ambition, and wants security above all.

Theory Y, in contrast, includes the following assumptions about human beings:

1. The expenditure of physical and mental effort in work is as natural as play or rest.
2. Human beings will exercise self-direction and self-control in the service of objectives to which they are committed.
3. The average person learns, under proper conditions, not only to accept but also to seek responsibility.

Using McGregor's terms as opposing alternatives, we can create the following continuum:

Theory X • • • • • • Theory Y

Which theory corresponds most closely to your assumptions about individuals in organizations? Perhaps we should ask, "Which set of assumptions is compatible with your view of yourself?" and, "Are others in organizations really that different?" You can also ask the four questions that were developed earlier about assumptions.

James O'Toole, in *Vanguard Management*, lists four assumptions about workers that James Renier wanted Honeywell managers to accept:

1. People want to do a good job.
2. Each employee knows how to do his or her own job better than anyone else.
3. Employees deserve to be recognized as intelligent, responsible people who can contribute to decisions that affect their work.
4. People need information so that they can better understand the goals and problems of the organization and make informed decisions [1985, p. 129].

If managers share these assumptions, which resemble Theory Y assumptions, and share the value of high productivity, then it may seem that the organization would have a strong culture with few disagreements. Assumptions about individuals, however, pertain to only one aspect of organizational life. Another and equally important aspect is our assumptions about the organization's system, or community. We can explore these assumptions in regard to a shared value of fairness or justice:

We may value justice, but we have different assumptions about how to achieve it.

Suppose that a group agrees that people should be treated fairly and also sees instances of unfairness. So it agrees that something should be done. Some in the group assume that the way to achieve justice is through the imposition of rules. Others assume that justice and therefore fair treatment only come about when people feel related to each other, or become a "community." These different assumptions would support very different policies. The first supports the development of guidelines for correct behavior and perhaps a system of punishment for those who act unjustly toward others. The second would probably lead to policies that would encourage interaction among persons in the organization, because through such interaction members could become aware of the impact that injustice had on others as well as on the organization itself. The continuum for these assumptions would look like the following:

Rule justice • • • • Community justice

These two assumptions parallel Boulding's (1970) organizers of threat and integration but leave out his third organizer: exchange. The exchange organizer can help us analyze our assumptions about how to achieve excellence:

> We may value excellence but have different
> assumptions about how to achieve it.

Assumptions about how to achieve excellence center around our understanding of the meaning of work. For some, meaningful work entails a fair return on one's investment. Perhaps no one has expressed this assumption as strongly as Ayn Rand.

> The symbol of all relationships among such men
> [rational men], the moral symbol of respect for human beings, is *the trader*. We, who live by values,
> not by loot, are traders, both in matter and in spirit.
> A trader is a man who earns what he gets and does
> not give or take the undeserved. A trader does not
> ask to be paid for his failures, nor does he ask to

be loved for his flaws. A trader does not squander his body as fodder or his soul as alms. Just as he does not give his work except in trade for material values, so he does not give the values of his spirit — his love, his friendship, his esteem — except in payment and in trade for human virtues, in payment for his own selfish pleasure, which he receives from men he can respect [1961, p. 133].

Rand's glorification of the trader shows us what happens when we take one aspect of human relationships — especially of work relationships — and remove it from its larger context. Although relationships of exchange constitute one aspect of organizational relationships, persons do not relate only through exchange but also through what they can do together. Most organizations, as networks of persons, involve not only systems of exchange but also, as Kenneth Boulding has argued, systems of integration and threat.

The case discussed earlier about temporary workers illustrates the validity and also the danger of emphasizing exchange relations. Temporary employees do not see themselves, nor are they seen by others, as members of the organization. They trade their work for wages and remain excluded, in many cases, not only from company benefits but also from discussions about the future of the organization. In other words, they take for granted the system of integration that provides the essential agreements for trade to take place. Such systems of exchange live off and can eventually deplete the system of integration, which can lead to a weakening of the organization itself. The activity of belonging to an organization includes much more than trading service for wages.

Much of the meaning of our work depends on the quantity and quality of exchange relationships. The wages or salary received in return for our work certainly give it meaning, especially in a context where money signals worth. The "buyer," however, is not the only measure of our work's meaning. The phenomenon of production is essentially a human activity — a definition of the self in the activity of making. Therefore, its value depends not only on the evaluation by its consumer but also on our mutual recognition of each other as centers of meaning.

In her influential study *The Human Condition,* Hannah Arendt distinguished between three basic human activities: labor, work, and acting/speaking (1959, p. 9). She speaks of the labor of the body, the work of the hands, and the acting/speaking of the person. We labor, or others labor for us, to meet the necessities of life. We work to fabricate a world fit to live in, and we act and speak to appear as humans in the world we have created. In organizational life, we work as producers but also live as participants who desire recognition as actors in an organization's life.

One of the most profound analyses of the complexity of working in organizations still remains Karl Marx's discussion of alienation. Essentially, alienation occurs when persons become separated from their basic humanness and become commodities—things to be bought and sold. They even experience self-alienation as they treat themselves as things. "The *value* of the worker as capital rises according to demand and supply, and even *physically* his *existence,* his life, was and is looked upon as a supply of a commodity like any other. . . . Production does not simply produce man as a commodity, the *human commodity,* man in the role of *commodity;* it produces him in keeping with this role, as a *mentally* and physically *dehumanized* being" ([1844] 1971, p. 120). In alienated environments, the "meaning" of work becomes a meaning separated from the basic human process of living and becomes a substitute for it. Persons are seen as "replaceable" because they serve only as commodities for the system of production. They are, to use Rand's terms, things to be traded.

When we consider the meaning of work, a Marxist analysis of alienation asks us to think about the contradiction between ourselves as traders existing in relationships of exchange and ourselves as self-producers who become what we make of ourselves. To use terms that remind us of Kantian ethics, we can ask whether we see each other at work as traders, persons for a price, or as actors, persons with a dignity. To use another set of terms, we can distinguish between seeing workers as having intrinsic value or as having instrumental value. We can locate these as the opposing alternatives in our next continuum:

Instrumental • • • • • • Intrinsic

The options between these two extremes allow us to ask such questions as: What value do you place on your work? What is it worth to you personally? Financially? Socially? Does the exchange transaction show respect for what you have invested of yourself in your productivity? What significance do you place on the results of your work? Does the organization's use of your "product" respect the value of your being?

How you answer these questions depends not only on your view of human relationships but also on your assumptions about the character of organizations. Although organizational life has been analyzed throughout this book, we need a way to analyze our assumptions about its nature:

> We may agree that organizations should be responsible but have different assumptions about their nature.

Gareth Morgan's *Images of Organization* (1986) reviews eight different "images of organizations," which include seeing the organization as a machine, an organism, a brain, a culture, a political system, a psychic prison, a flux, and an instrument of domination. Drawing on Morgan's work as well as his own analysis, Stephen Robbins lists the following ten interpretations of organizations:

1. *Rational entities in pursuit of goals* — Organizations exist to achieve goals, and the behavior of organizational members can be explained as the rational pursuit of these goals.
2. *Coalitions of powerful constituencies* — Organizations are made up of groups, each of which seeks to satisfy its own self-interest. These groups use their power to influence the distribution of resources within the organization.

3. *Open systems* — Organizations are input-output transformation systems that depend on their environment for survival.

4. *Meaning-producing systems* — Organizations are artificially created entities. Their goals and purposes are symbolically created and maintained by management.

5. *Loosely coupled systems* — Organizations are made up of relatively independent units that can pursue dissimilar or even conflicting goals.

6. *Political systems* — Organizations are composed of internal constituencies that seek control over the decision process in order to enhance their position.

7. *Instruments of domination* — Organizations place members into job "boxes" that constrain what they can do and individuals with whom they can interact. Additionally, they are given a boss who has authority over them.

8. *Information-processing units* — Organizations interpret their environment, coordinate activities, and facilitate decision making by processing information horizontally and vertically through a structural hierarchy.

9. *Psychic prisons* — Organizations constrain members by constructing job descriptions, departments, divisions, and standards of acceptable and unacceptable behaviors. When accepted by members, they become artificial barriers that limit choices.

10. *Social contracts* — Organizations are composed of sets of unwritten agreements whereby members perform certain behaviors in return for compensation [Stephen P. Robbins, *Organization Theory: Structure, Design, and Applications,* 2e, © 1987, p. 9. Reprinted by permission of Prentice Hall, Inc. Englewood Cliffs, New Jersey.].

When we review the many different kinds of organizations, we can probably find some that will fit each of these images. Most organizations can probably accommodate more than one. The above list contains some views that certainly conflict, yet the conflict may not require an either-or choice. Chapter Seven, for example, assumed that organizations could be interpreted as moral communities and as systems. These two assumptions appear contradictory. The systems approach tends to view persons as merely functionaries of the system, as parts coordinated for the total functioning of the system. The moral community approach, in contrast, emphasizes the moral worth of individuals — their autonomy as participants in the decision-making process. Instead of interpreting these two assumptions as mutually exclusive, however, they were treated as complementary.

Instead of arguing that we must choose either the moral community approach or a systems approach, I have emphasized a pluralistic approach that allows different perspectives where each perspective offers some truth about organizations but no perspective offers the whole truth.

The acceptance of complementarity allows us to entertain different assumptions about organizations and therefore to increase our resources for making decisions. It highlights one of the major themes of this book — differences should be seen as resources. Differences in our assumptions about organizations probably involve several points of reference rather than a simple alternative, so the rectangle in Figure 19 contains four images that should help us to assess them.

Where would we place our organization on this quadrant? Perhaps it is more appropriate to draw some sort of loop in the center of the square that would set the boundaries between the four alternatives.

When we examine assumptions, we will find differences, and these differences must be resolved or they will limit the group's success. Differences on the level of assumptions can, of course, add to the learning possibilities of a group if the group is open to change. If it is not, the different assumptions will probably prevent the members from reaching an agreement on either a policy or a redesign of an organization's system. When we find differences in values, however, we do have other possibilities.

Figure 19.

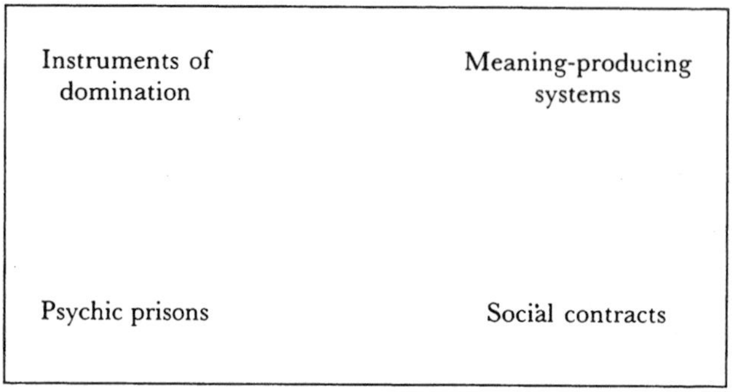

Instruments of domination	Meaning-producing systems
Psychic prisons	Social contracts

Sometimes, the presence of common assumptions may allow compromise and trade-offs, because the assumptions represent an agreeable context for the disagreeable values or interests.

Different Values and Shared Assumptions

Situations where people or groups share assumptions but have different values are found daily in most organizations. For example, a list of the various stakeholders and their primary values in most corporate systems would look something like Table 1.

Table 1.

Owners	Workers	Consumers	Citizens
Profit	Wages	Quality	Prosperity
Quality	Working conditions	Fair prices	Employment
Working conditions	Quality	Service	Tax revenue
Wages	Profit	Style	Stability

The lists in the table show some shared values, but the different groups give them different priority. We also see some different values. Can these different groups work together to realize their values? If they share similar assumptions about the organization as a system, about mutual interdependence and growth, and about the organization as a community, where all are members, then they can make the compromises and trade-offs necessary for resolving conflicting values.

If wage earners and managers, for example, have different values in terms of a wage increase, they will much more likely come to a compromise that both can accept if they share assumptions about the meaning of work or the significance of participation than if they do not. With common assumptions, we can work with differences in interests, differences that probably cannot be avoided in our socioeconomic system. We can now consider two cases of different values and shared assumptions. The first case begins with the following statement:

Some people value higher wages (wealth) and others more security (benefits), but they share the assumption that one's work should enhance one's self-esteem.

The question for this group, of course, is whether the assumption of self-esteem can provide a basis for trade-offs between the different values of wealth and security. It depends, at least at first glance, on the degree to which these values serve as necessary conditions for self-esteem. Perhaps instead of being necessary they are only sufficient. To pursue this line of thought, we need to clarify the difference between necessary and sufficient conditions.

Necessary conditions are required for some event or state of affairs to happen. The presence of oxygen, for example, is a necessary condition for fire. No oxygen, no fire. In other words, there is fire only if there is oxygen. Sufficient conditions are enough to make something happen. Gas and a match, for example, are sufficient for starting a fire, but then so are kindling and a match. Neither one is necessary; you could also start a fire with other combustible materials. How does the difference between necessary conditions and sufficient conditions relate to values and assumptions?

Values may be either necessary or sufficient conditions for one's assumptions. In this case, we can ask if wealth is a necessary and/or sufficient condition for self-esteem. Some may assume that it is sufficient. High wages, in other words, will increase one's self-esteem, but so might security or a number of other values such as recognition. So while they might be sufficient, they may not be necessary. If neither wealth nor security is a necessary condition, then it is possible to place both in a larger package of sufficient conditions for self-esteem and develop a policy that balances them in some fashion. Each receives some of what she or he values and also receives other parts of the package, so everyone comes away affirming their basic assumption about what people need.

As this case demonstrates, some assumptions can be used as a primary value to negotiate among other secondary values. Other assumptions require a different type of analysis:

> We may disagree about the right of employees
> to information about their organization's
> future plans, but we also hold the assumption
> that "what goes around, comes around."

"What goes around, comes around" signals a common assumption that the quality of our conduct affects the quality of our lives. People who always manipulate situations finally find themselves suffering the manipulation of others. People who help others receive help, too. An opposing assumption is that our acts' consequences will not affect the conditions of our lives. If we all agree that "what goes around, comes around," then we have a basis for dealing with the different notions of the value of information. We could argue in two different ways. To refute those who want to withhold information, we could argue that the act of withholding will eventually return with unpleasant consequences such as lower productivity. For those who want to receive the information, we could argue that without it, they cannot understand what is changing their conditions and therefore cannot create the best conditions possible. If unknown events shape their conditions, then the link between acts and consequences remains a mystery. Without this information, they cannot become responsible for their decisions. These arguments may not convince everyone, but they illustrate how shared assumptions can serve as a basis for evaluating the merits of different value judgments.

Both of these examples of shared assumptions and different values have looked for ways to use assumptions to discover the right thing to do. If we acknowledge that different groups within an organization's total system — owners, consumers, managers, workers, and citizens — have different interests, then instead of arguing for a strong organizational ideology that suppresses these differences, we can argue for their participation so that the differences can be used to develop more resources to evaluate policy proposals. Different interests, however, do not automatically signal different assumptions. If the different interests can be grounded in common assumptions, successful negotiation between them becomes more likely than when the assumptions are ignored and the group remains stuck on the level of different values.

Analyzing assumptions can become a very effective means of developing the basis for reconciling differences, or at least for understanding them. The worksheet in Exhibit 8 in Chapter Eleven offers an opportunity for individuals or groups to examine their assumptions about the aspects of organizational culture discussion in this chapter. Engaging in this type of analysis with a group considering different proposals requires a commitment to vigorous communication. If we assume that communication can make no difference, then we have no reason for practicing ethical reflection. Chapter Ten will provide some strategies for evaluating our assumptions about communication in organizations.

Chapter Ten

Establishing Responsible Communication Habits

Organizational power, guided by notions of justice and rights, provides the organization with possibilities for moral action. To realize these possibilities, organizational members must have times and places where they can engage in ethical reflection. They need communicative situations that can handle controversy, the analysis of value judgments and assumptions, and the negotiation of differences. Whether an organization possesses such situations depends on its everyday culture and the assumptions of its members.

Our assumptions about communicative possibilities affect the whole organization. As Katz and Kahn have argued, "communication — the exchange of information and the transmission of meaning — is the very essence of a social system or an organization" (1978, p. 428). Communication patterns and practices keep the whole organization organized. Few questions, therefore, are more important than the questions that allow us to understand an organization's communicative practices.

Organizations are comprised of a vast array of parts. These parts represent different tasks, work routines, technologies, and departments. People who work in them come with different values, career plans, training, and capacities. As they take up their roles in the organization, they also begin to take on the roles' perspectives, goals, and interests. Furthermore, in the dynamics of organizational life, people in the different parts of the organization experience different changes, receive different information, and develop their own learning styles. All of these factors tend to fragment the organization into specialized groups with different communicative patterns. While the organizational charts may show how the organizational groups fit together, charts can never unite these differences. Organizational integration ultimately depends on the continuing conversations of all members. An organization's unity ultimately depends on its members' assumptions about communication.

We could assume that the organizational culture and structure controls the organization's communication patterns. In traditional organizational charts, the "flow of information" moves from the top to the bottom. Even in more horizontal structures, patterns of communication develop that turn the discussion in specific directions. Because we cannot say everything at once, every conversation takes up some aspects of the total context and excludes others. These patterns can become so routine and habitual that people blindly follow them. They no longer perceive the distinction between what is said and what should be said. Patterns of expectations determine who speaks and what is said. As an organization continues its everyday life, as its "themes" are further developed, members tend to develop a kind of "blindness" to those aspects of situations that lie beyond their everyday conversations.

Organizations not only structure the patterns of communication, but also influence our attitude toward language. Conversations usually focus on how to get things done, and we use language as a tool to achieve that end. An organizational frame of mind prompts us to see language as a *thing* to be handled and manipulated. Language, in other words, is taken as a property that belongs to the organization.

Instead of assuming that language belongs to the organization, we could also assume just the opposite: organizations belong to language. Admittedly, organizations do influence our terminology and our communication structures, but even more profoundly, our communications structure organizations. Organizational life, therefore, ultimately depends on our use of language. Instead of information flowing through an organization, organizations flow in the stream of human discourse. Language in all its diversity and dialects provides a necessary network between the individuals and the organization as well as between organizations and the public. Language, however, ultimately belongs to the continued conversation of men and women with the potential to ask new questions, voice new insights, and develop new arguments. Language, in other words, is grounded in an organization's moral community even more profoundly than it is shaped and developed by an organization's systems.

To understand the dynamics of language, we need to recognize that every time we think or speak, we exhibit both our individuality and our sociality. Speaking involves participating in a particular language — we never speak language itself but always some cultural language such as English, Japanese, or German. We even speak the language of our subcultures and of our organizational culture. Language is a cultural product. At the same time, speaking is how we express our individuality, even our special creativity. What one person says uniquely expresses that person. Each person is known as someone rather than merely as a member of a group because we participate individually in the act of languaging, if I may use such an expression. This dynamic of language gives us possibilities of saying what needs to be said about what needs to be done.

Responsible Communication

For organizations to realize their possibilities for ethical reflection, they need to develop communication expectations that correspond to their members' responsibilities. Responsibility requires power — we need the power to respond — it also requires language — the articulation of our response. Organizations actually have two fundamental activities that make ethics possible and necessary: their power and their language. The use of language — the activity of communication — allows men and women to create and maintain an organization. Power — the ability to influence and to coerce — develops as the organization grows and diversifies. All the parts of the organization become potential centers of power that can either create or prevent organizational change and renewal.

Discourse can empower individuals and groups because discourse brings organizations into being and maintains them. If you change the language, the constituency of the audience, the means of argumentation, you change the organization. People are discovering that increased participation in management results in new communities of power. Many others experience that the lack of a communicating community leaves them alone and powerless. Organizations must talk to survive and to grow. Who is included in their conversation, how the participants talk to each other, and what they have to say will finally determine whether any organization will become responsible or not.

To discuss ethical issues in organizations, people have to raise questions that direct groups toward the ethical dimensions of their work. The responsibility for doing this, however, not only rests with individuals; it also depends on the group and on the group's communication habits. Actually, we must consider the mutual interdependence of the competence of individuals to communicate and a group's patterns of communication. Most of us have observed that it seems easier for some individuals to raise ethical questions than for others, but we have also observed that some settings seem more amiable to ethical discussions than are others. We need to develop some criteria to tell the difference between such settings and then to develop strategies to bring about those conditions that allow responsible communication.

Dimensions of Communication Practices

Just as raising ethical questions seems much easier for some individuals than for others, it seems much easier in some groups than in others to ask about values, responsibilities, or obligations. Like individuals, groups have developed habits from their experiences and expectations. These habits tend to focus on some aspects of reality, ignoring others. As we go through a day or a week, most of us move in and out of groups with different communication habits. If you consider the different groups you belong to and ask how easy it is to talk about values, purposes, justice, or responsible actions in each of these settings, you will probably find a variety of communication habits. To analyze differences in groups further and to provide conceptual tools for discussing these differences, we can use the following seven considerations about communication settings:

1. Range of topics
2. Purpose of meeting
3. Equality of communication
4. Oral and written traditions
5. Dimensions of meaning
6. Degree of involvement
7. Personal presence

Each of these considerations can be placed on a continuum, much as we did earlier with basic assumptions, so that we can better understand our own communication expectations in various communication settings.

Range of Topics. The range of the communication refers to the number of topics or subjects that can easily be discussed. Some groups expect only specific items on the agenda, while in other groups nothing seems inappropriate. For example, people may structure a meeting for employee evaluation so that participants expect to discuss performance but not the work environment, the organization's future, or the employee's career plans. On the one hand, some boundaries may be completely justified, because we cannot discuss everything at every meeting. On the other hand, restricting the range of topics discussed can prevent persons from understanding each other and developments in their workplace. Settings that habitually accept more topics will probably encourage participants to raise unexpected questions and offer innovative perceptions. To analyze a particular communicative setting, you can use the following continuum to evaluate whether you think it encourages a wide range of topics or only very few:

Many topics   •   •   •   •   •   Few topics

If you find that few topics can easily be discussed, then sharing your evaluation may help to broaden the boundaries, if they need broadening. For ethical analysis, participants need the freedom to ask questions that will raise new issues, so at least some groups should expect such questions.

Purpose of Meeting. Most meetings have particular tasks to accomplish or problems to solve, but in the process members also perform other communicative functions; they talk about specific topics and they talk about them with others. These two purposes can be understood as exchanging information and developing relations. Sometimes, developing the relationship seems to take precedence, while in other settings — such as when we ask for specific directions — we just want correct information.

Any organization, of course, needs "informational meetings." These meetings, however, rely on human relations that provide the background and the context for the transmission of information. In some cases, even though the participants are tacitly aware of fractures in their relationships, they keep talking on the level of transmitting information. Bringing up the relational issue seems out of place. To accomplish the meeting's task, they stay in character even though their particular character or role within the organization conflicts with what is actually happening between real persons.

Many of our meetings balance sharing information and developing relationships. Those that emphasize one and ignore the other finally become dysfunctional. Sharing information by itself feeds on the background of good relations but does not replenish it. When this background is depleted, then participants will no longer have the mutual trust necessary to grant to each other their cooperation. At the other extreme, an exclusive focus on relationships can prevent the group from accomplishing its tasks. To see if a particular communicative setting has the proper balance, you can evaluate it on the following continuum:

Relational • • • • • • Informational

Meetings that are primarily informational, as you would expect, will not give much latitude for participants to develop the kind of rapport necessary for critical analysis of value judgments and assumptions. Neither will meetings dominated by maintaining close relationships provide this freedom. The inclusion of *both* group dynamics — especially in groups that continue to work together over a period of time — will be necessary for effective ethical reflection.

Equality of Communication. Because not everyone has the same place, position, or responsibility in an organization, thinking about equality needs to begin by remembering its first principle: to treat equals equally and unequals unequally. As we learned in Chapter Eight, organizations structure inequality. People differ in their responsibilities, levels of control, and accountability. Some have more, or at least different, knowledge than others. These differences, however, do not necessarily prevent persons from feeling of equal worth in their discussions. It depends on how we interpret not only the differences but also the similarities.

People do experience significant similarities with others who are also quite different. Parents and children, for example, can find similarities as family members and experience a basic equality even though they have different roles and responsibilities. Persons in organizations can find similarities, too, and when these similarities are relevant to the issue, then one should expect "equal treatment." In other words, the structure of hierarchical relationships does not necessarily mean an unequal communication pattern. If the participants expect that their experience and their ideas have the same value as those of anyone else and expect mutual respect from others, then the hierarchical structure will become irrelevant. The feeling that "my supervisor always talks down to me" is a good indication of unequal communication. Such feelings usually force participants to fight for recognition before they can say what needs to be said. Many times we never move past the fight. In fact, in some cases, the hierarchical habit of communication itself becomes the significant issue because it shows a disrespect for the moral agency of others. Robert Terry offers a communicative imperative that addresses this issue: "To be just is to guarantee for others the implicit values one necessarily claims for oneself in the communicative act" (1970, pp. 34–35). To evaluate the equality of the relationships in a particular communicative setting, especially when you imagine raising issues about the performance of the organization or analyzing what should be done, you can use the following continuum:

Equal • • • • • • • Unequal

Oral and Written Traditions. Our next aspect of communication involves what can be called its tradition. For example, some communications between persons in organizations rest on memos and written messages. Instead of face-to-face discussions, people carry on a "dialogue" through the receiving and giving of written messages. The experiences of reading and writing largely define this tradition. Contemporary business writing's emphasis on standard formats and brevity tends toward an "economical" and instrumental communication, with a very thin texture. In contrast to this written tradition, the oral tradition has a rich, textured background based on common experiences, stories, and sayings. Instead of the explicit references that are necessary in written communication, people can make many more implicit references in an oral tradition. The oral tradition also allows more personal involvement and therefore appears much less controlled and ordered than the written tradition.

As we move among the various communicative settings at and outside of work, we also move through settings that belong more to an oral or more to a written tradition. With family, old friends, and even long-term co-workers, we can rely on common experiences and earlier events to provide a textured context for current discussions. These settings belong more to an oral tradition. In highly structured organizational settings, in contrast, we find ourselves living much more in a tradition of writing. In many cases, of course, we can see both traditions. To evaluate which tradition a particular communicative setting belongs to, you can use the following continuum:

Oral tradition • • • • Written tradition

Because ethical analysis involves the examination of implied value judgments and assumptions, this continuum will help you know how much you can count on a similar background and implicit agreements about how things work.

Dimensions of Meaning. To understand this aspect of our communication patterns, we can turn to the history of the interpretation of texts. During the Middle Ages, scholars used what they called the "fourfold" method of interpreting. Each text (scholars were primarily concerned with biblical texts) had, in other words, four different meanings. These were the literal, which indicated what actually happened; the allegorical, which stated what we should believe; the moral, which gave rules for daily life; and the analogical, which expressed the future state of things. As the Middle Ages gave way to the Renaissance and then to the early modern period, an emphasis on the literal interpretation replaced the fourfold method, and, especially with the rise of pietism in the seventeenth century, people began to speak of the one and only one meaning of texts.

Whether a text has multiple meanings or a single meaning depends on the expectations of the interpreter and the community of interpretation much more than it depends on the text itself. For centuries, readers expected multiple dimensions, and now many expect only one. When we share in communicative activities today, we also have expectations that condition the various dimensions we can "hear" and therefore respond to.

At the one extreme are instances of one-dimensionality, in which the communication only means one thing: "Take the next turn to the left." At other times, we can easily interpret various meanings in a discussion: "If you don't do some more training, you will probably not receive a promotion" may be taken literally, but it can also mean something about an organization's reward system, one's career plans, and one's values and assumptions about how things work.

Discussions that develop expectations toward literal interpretations without a tacit acknowledgment of other dimensions of meaning can inhibit ethical questions, because ethical reflection requires at least two dimensions such as a difference between what is happening and what ought to happen. Actually, since ethical analysis requires that we have access to implied value judgments and assumptions, it requires a multidimensional communication. Such discourse not only includes space for ethical questions but also allows participants to use different modes of discourse such as riddles, stories, and jokes. Sometimes we can gauge the dimensionality of a group's communication habit by the presence and diversity of humor. In such settings, we can express ambiguity, doubt, and opposing views. Whereas one-dimensional communication controls the meaning level by the authority of literalism, multidimensional communication delights in innuendo and metaphorical or symbolic references. You can evaluate your selected communicative setting on the following continuum from multidimensional to one-dimensional:

Multidimensional   •   •   •   One-dimensional

Degree of Involvement. As we move through these categories — range, purpose, equality, orality, and dimensions — it becomes clear that one overriding consideration is the degree of personal involvement a group expects. Personal involvement refers to our stake in the outcome of a conversation (its meaning for us) and our exposure of ourselves. Sometimes, what happens does matter to us, and we communicate so that our feelings and interests become apparent. This is probably more true in family relationships and friendships than in work relationships. Other times, even though the conversation does matter to us, we remain detached. In some professions, a detached attitude has been perceived as necessary. Medical doctors, for example, learn to develop a "detached concern" for a patient. At its best this posture shows a caring that is channeled into professional competence, but at its worst it represents an objectification of others that treats them as things. Most communication in organizations seeks a balance between limiting personal involvement, on the one hand, so that personal differences do not block cooperation, and yet, on the other hand, encouraging personal involvement to maintain motivation and morale. When we think of different communicative situations, however, we probably will find that we are much more involved in some situations than in others.

Ethical conversations depend on people caring about what happens. They do require personal involvement. Total involvement, however, can lead to moralistic responses that prevent participants from engaging in ethical reflection about the strengths and weaknesses of different views. The move from moral response to ethical reflection requires a movement from one's personal response to an analysis of it. You can use the following continuum to evaluate your personal involvement, and that of others, in particular communicative settings:

Involved • • • • • • • Detached

Personal Presence. Personal presence in a group can be seen in terms of a particular kind of personal power: a power integral to one's person — not the power of domination but of self-determination. Communications where people feel free to become expansive and to make gestures, to show themselves as particular individuals, would rank high on the scale of personal presence. In contrast, communicative patterns that encourage submission to authority or in other ways inhibit people would rank low. The presence of one's self may be hard to evaluate, and yet most of us have experienced times when our own presence seemed to make a difference and other times when it did not. The difference shows itself in levels of energy, and interaction, as well as in the degree of fun. If engaging in the process of ethical reflection empowers employees, then those situations where they already have some power will be more conducive to ethical reflection. You can measure your expectations of appearing strong or weak in a communicative setting on the following continuum:

Strong • • • • • • • • Weak

When we evaluate one particular communication situation on the basis of these seven aspects of communication, we can gain some valuable information about its possibilities and limitations for ethical reflection. When we compare and contrast several different situations, the seven continuums can help us understand why one situation has more possibilities than another. To evaluate different communicative situations in your organization, you can use the worksheet in Exhibit 9 in Chapter Eleven.

Most people do engage in different patterns of communication with different individuals, groups, and in different situations, which probably represents a healthy pluralism. For an organization to realize its possibilities as a responsible community, members must create situations in which they have opportunities to consider value judgments and assumptions in the process of making decisions. The next chapter explores some of the conditions that are necessary for this to happen.

Chapter Eleven

Creating Conditions for Ethical Reflection in Organizations

To practice ethical reflection in organizations, we need the right conditions and some training. We do not need to introduce anything totally foreign into organizational life. People in organizations already use their value judgments and assumptions in making decisions. In many cases, they already consider alternative courses of action and opposing views. Sometimes they consider the mutual interdependence of an organization's different components and evaluate whether its structures treat persons fairly. Representatives of the various stakeholders already disagree with each other and yet also find some things on which they agree. So when we think about ethical reflection in organizations, we do not have to bring something new into them because the issues, disagreements, value judgments, and assumptions are already there. We just have to develop a conscious process of making explicit the operative value judgments and assumptions, of evaluating them with appropriate ethical criteria, and of talking together in a well-designed, just system that respects human rights. For this to occur, several conditions should be considered.

The first and primary condition for ethical reflection is the organization's moral community and the moral life of its members and constituencies. How we live with ourselves, others, and our environment constitutes our moral life. Our morality refers to our characteristic (character) ways of acting and responding to situations and activities. Some acts outrage us, bring us happiness, or lift our spirits. We certainly make moral decisions when we immediately respond with our whole selves to possibilities of good or evil. This activity represents our moral life.

In many ways, our moral life is given to us. We are born into moral communities and these communities give us our moral attitudes. As we become mature, we gain more control over our moral life, even though it always bears the mark of our personal story, family life, and culture.

Ethics arises out of and depends on and yet has a certain independence from our moral life. The independence of ethics comes from the act of reflection — of thinking about our moral responses to situations. To think about the moral life involves an act of withdrawing from it and making it an object of thought. So, our moral life gives us something to think about. Through our emotional response to situations and to others, we define not only the significance of issues but also what we should do. In some cases, of course, our moral responses suffice, but in others, either when we find ourselves unsure or in disagreement with others, we need to reflect on our responses and our decisions.

Although our moral convictions and responses give ethical reflection something to reflect on, they do not completely direct our reflections, nor do they provide all we need to understand situations or to discover the best course of action. In fact, moral convictions can hinder ethical reflection when they become absolutist and can turn any difference of opinion into a contest of good and evil. Ethical reflection requires moral convictions to begin with and yet, at the same time, distance from them to think about them. Especially in group settings, people need to respect each other's moral responses but need also to move beyond them to ethical reflection. The purpose of ethical reflection is not to directly change the morals of individuals but rather to make the best decisions possible. The process may change participants' morals, but that is a by-product of the process, not its purpose.

Ethical reflection always occurs in particular situations, and, as was shown in Chapter Nine, some situations are more open for reflection than others are. Some organizational cultures assume that truth is discovered or revealed through authority or dogma, while others assume that truth emerges through the give-and-take of debate. Ethical reflection, especially when it entertains opposing views, will be much more difficult to develop for the former than for the latter. Still, most organizational cultures are not one-dimensional. Once discussions begin, important information and interpretations become available. If ethical reflection does not happen in an organization, it is not because there is nothing to reflect on. Perhaps members do not have the skills, conceptual tools, and training in ethical reflection. Perhaps the organization itself is not conducive to such discussions. It may lack the conditions that allow organizational members to actually engage in ethical reflection. In some cases, schedule and time restraints may pose a problem. Although these constraints must be acknowledged, they can also be managed. People usually find time to do what is worth doing, and once ethical reflection becomes recognized as a necessary means for making the best decisions and preventing moral mistakes, the scheduling problems will probably find a quick solution.

Ethical reflection should not be seen as some isolated activity apart from the regular processes of making decisions. Instead, ethical reflection belongs within the already established decision-making processes, in dialogue with other types of methods for deciding what should be done. While the physical constraints must be considered, they probably will not deter effective ethical reflection, nor will they alone facilitate it. Ethical reflection needs much more than a room and a block of time. Before people will share their own value judgments and assumptions and engage in argumentative analysis, they need to develop some common agreements and expectations or communicative conditions. Probably the most basic conditions center around issues of power.

Condition of Power

The condition of power relates to both the participants and the ethical process itself as part of an organizational system. For ethical reflection to be effective and to actually elicit participation, the process itself must be empowered, which in turn empowers those who engage in it. As was shown in Chapter Eight, powers can also be understood as rights, and here it is possible to speak of the rights of participants as a way of determining the powers to which they are entitled. These rights include the right to relevant information, the right to assembly, and the right to free speech — all of which are rights that can be justified not only by roles and relations within organizations, but also in terms of basic human rights. The rights needed for effective ethical reflection are not extraordinary but rather only the ordinary rights of every person. At the same time, these rights need to be acknowledged in the organizational context. As was indicated in Chapter Eight, combining justice and rights allows us to more fully understand the meaning of each one. Participating in ethical reflection does not give members powers that cannot be justified by rights and justice, but neither should members be denied powers that can be justified. The tasks assigned to the process of ethical reflection will usually be particular issues or questions that need answers. In such a context, the right to free speech is not the right to say anything but the right to say what is needed. Likewise, the right to information is not the right to whatever one would like to know but to what one needs to know to understand not only what to decide but also the consequences of one's decision. These limits on speech and information follow from the resources that the organization has to distribute and the criteria of distribution — for example, that free speech would be distributed equally and according to contribution, and information on the basis of need. Members must be empowered, but that empowerment must also be justified by the social meaning of the resources they receive (justice) and the human meaning of their work (rights).

Another aspect of the condition of power we need to consider is how ethics fits into organizational systems. The previous discussion (Chapter Seven) of Galbraith's and Boulding's analyses of the sources and instruments of power and the organizers of systems can help us understand what is at stake here. Taken together, their theories provide us with the choices of (1) an organizational ethics that belongs to the systems of threat and personality and uses the instrument of punishment, (2) an organizational ethics that belongs to the systems of exchange and property and uses the instruments of compensation, or (3) an organizational ethics that belongs to systems of integration and organizations and uses the instruments of conditioning or belief. An ethical practice that attempts to control the behavior of persons and uses threats of punishment as its basic means of achieving its goals would conform to the first alternative. Some do use ethics in this manner, but throughout this book I have argued against this use as the primary intent of ethics, although recognizing that punishment is sometimes necessary to maintain community or to protect others from harm. The threat of punishment has probably been necessary, for example, to encourage some corporations to stop polluting the environment. In any case, this ethics has limited value because in the long run it destroys the very cooperation it requires to succeed. The second alternative of placing ethics in the system of property and exchange would see ethics as an instrument for protecting property and ensuring just exchanges. Such an ethics also has value, but ethics remains very precarious here because it usually gets used to protect those with property from those without property. For an organizational ethics, it makes sense to place ethical refection in the system of integration and to see its primary power as that of developing and evaluating beliefs. Since the process of ethical reflection concerns the analysis of value judgments and assumptions used in the process of decision making as well as the analysis of systems in terms of the meaning of social goods (justice) and the meaning of human life (rights), the real home for a powerful ethic is in an organization's system of integration. Ethics should be a power to unite organizations, even as it helps members to discover and deal with their differences. In fact, only if it really belongs to this system and is experienced as such by organizational members will it have a chance of fulfilling its mission of enabling organizational responsibility.

Besides the appropriate conditions of power relations between the participants and other aspects and subsystems of the organizations, several other considerations are necessary for the process of ethical reflection. Perhaps the most significant is the condition of trust.

Condition of Trust

If participants are really to disagree or to analyze their own and each other's value judgments and assumptions, they have to trust one another. To increase the group's understanding of the issues, the organization, and themselves, they must feel confident that the increased understanding will not be used to their disadvantage. All participants must agree that the understanding attained will be applied only to the issue under discussion, not to extraneous matters. Participants also need to believe that the discussion itself will be fair. A fair discussion requires that the most persuasive arguments that the group develops will carry the day.

But what kind of arguments should be persuasive for ethical reflection? We can answer this question by using the classical rhetorical terms of *ethos, logos,* and *pathos* as the three elements of a speech. Ethos refers to the presented character of the speaker. Arguments from ethos find their power in a person's status. The expert, who argues that his views are correct because he is an expert, uses an ethos argument. Logos arguments rely on the rationality of the argument — the strength of the connections between propositions. Our argumentative model relies on the logos element of a speech. Pathos, the third element of a speech, refers to the beliefs of the audience, especially those they hold dearly. Although all three have a place in a speech, most speeches emphasize one over the others. Advertisements with famous stars or athletes selling products, for example, depend almost solely on ethos arguments. Appeals for contributions to needy causes, in contrast, largely appeal to our emotions (pathos).

Actually, we find few examples today of arguments that rely on rationality (logos) in public life. Even in the citadels of democracy, our legislators mostly make appeals either to their own character or to the public's fears or desires. We are constantly in danger of making all speaking either a form of emotional expression or, even worse, entertainment. In such a state of affairs, only those who can entertain or pull the heartstrings can gain the stage, while those who think through the issues in terms of purpose, principle, or consequence seldom receive a hearing. Why should people give reasons when their persuasiveness can be overriden by either appeals to authority (ethos arguments) or appeals to emotionality (pathos arguments)? Only when group members can trust one another to actually listen and consider the merits of each other's thinking will people begin to reason together.

In the meeting of the consulting organization described in Chapter One, people felt free to express their feelings, but not to argue with one another. Perhaps the extensive expression of feelings so personalized the meeting that no one dared raise critical questions for fear of offending someone else. However, rationality alone, devoid of personal connections, cannot fulfill the requirements of ethical reflection. People need to think, but they need to think about their personal values and the group's values and beliefs. Good reasons include our personal responses, including our emotional responses, but only if they can be expressed and justified by our interpretation of the data and our assumptions. People have very good reasons to be angry, even outraged, as well as hurt or frustrated. The speaker's task is to demonstrate how the situation justified such a response rather than to let the emotional response serve as a justification for one's interpretation. The group does not have to avoid emotional responses but rather needs to bring them into the dialogue, discover their objective justifications, and then decide whether to agree or disagree with such an interpretation. Because organizational policy affects the well-being of people both inside and outside of the organization, ethical reflection should never become dominated by a calculating rationality. At the same time, it must promote a type of communication where people's private responses gain their validity in the group when they become part of public discourse — when they become available for inquiry and evaluation. Although it is difficult to inquire about emotional responses, at least in most organizational settings, it is not so difficult to inquire into the organizational conditions that justify them.

In summary, an emphasis on *ethos* turns the discussion

into an emphasis on a person's status. In such cases, who says something is more important than what is said. An emphasis on *pathos* turns the discussion into the expression of personal beliefs. In both of these instances, individual expressions overrun the possibilities of finding good reasons for the whole group. The process then becomes a contest of individual power rather than a process for group innovation. Participants can no longer trust the group's capacity to move together through the development of sound reasons for one policy or another. A respect for *logos,* in contrast, can ensure that good reasons will prevail.

Walzer's notion of justice can further our understanding of what trust means in ethical reflection because it allows us to evaluate whether a communicative situation is just. Walzer understood justice as the use of the appropriate criteria for the distribution of specific goods. These goods, moreover, had specific social meanings, which became the basis for the criteria of distribution. What goods are available for conversations about policy issues? Some of the goods include the chance to participate, attention from others, feedback, acceptance of ideas, and recognition. What criteria should we use to distribute these goods? We could give them to the most entertaining person, or to the one who makes us feel the best, or to the highest authority, or to the expert. But are these the correct criteria? Or do you agree that the chance to participate should be given to all who are affected by and have an interest in the issue? Should attention be given to those who have something significant to say? Should feedback be given to all active participants? Should acceptance also be given to all ideas that contribute to a group solution? Should recognition be given to those who both contribute to a group solution and can articulate good reasons that other members of the group can follow? These various criteria allow the distribution of the various goods entailed in decision making, and, at the same time, they set boundaries for what the group should not reward. If participants can count on the discussion distributing these goods by appropriate criteria, they will probably decide to become engaged in the process of ethical reflection.

Condition of Inclusion

How does one decide what groups should be part of the conversation? One answer is to examine who has a stake in the decision and to let these stakeholders constitute the conversation's participants. But who are the relevant stakeholders? Several years ago, a hospital went through an eighteen-month process of developing a new mission statement. During the process, it had involved all professional and staff groups at the hospital but not the local community. The hospital had not asked the community what kind of health care it wanted nor had it functioned as a listener in the deliberations. Why was a significant stakeholder left out? Partly because of oversight, partly because of a lack of structure to include the community. Mostly, the hospital probably did not think the community had any information the hospital did not already possess. But how did the hospital know this if it did not ask?

From the past decade of plant closures, we do know some of the stakeholders in corporations. They include numerous groups within the corporation, the region, the nation, and even beyond the nation. Should all these groups have a voice? Do workers in Mexico where a plant may be moved have a voice equal to that of workers in our local communities? These are difficult questions that remind us that the identification of groups must be accompanied by an examination of our common loyalties and communal responsibilities. Only when the relevant groups become involved in a decision-making process, either directly or indirectly, does it become possible to conduct an open and productive debate about such issues. Although not all stakeholders can always have physical representation in all processes of making decisions that affect them, a minimal condition is that they be taken into consideration. Without their knowledge and experience, a group cannot know what it is really doing. Actually, we benefit in two ways by including stakeholders. They present views we cannot know without them, and, by engaging in discussions with them, we can become aware of our own previously unknown assumptions. This use of stakeholders has been explored by Mason and Mitroff (1981), who show that different stakeholders can help to question strategic assumptions.

Condition of Role Flexibility

An old European tradition allowed the rulers to take on the role of peasants and the peasants to dress as kings for one day a year. Even if our organizations have moved beyond feudal forms of governance, switches in roles can still create significant insights. The conditions of role flexibility would humanize and even add humor to the decision-making process as well as bring new understanding to all. Especially when an individual participant has become strongly identified with one position or point of view, allowing him or her to take another position may not only provide a chance to see if the person understands the reasons for another position but also provides an opportunity to escape a social stereotype. This can be especially fruitful for someone who has become identified as the group's "moral critic." Although such individuals usually exhibit courage and sometimes sensitivity, they also can prevent other members from becoming involved in the critical process of reflection. Others can just wait for the moral critic to present the "bad news" and then feel satisfied that they have heard different sides. Sometimes, however, since the criticism has been so identified with a particular person, others never take it as something that they should consider. One means of moving out of this pattern is to assign different roles to participants. Let the "moral critic" defend the positive view, and let someone else play the critic. Since most of us probably acknowledge the strengths of different positions, encouraging persons to take on different roles will prevent the group from overpersonalizing what in fact are organizational issues.

Role flexibility can also work to provide the needed "space" for people to change their minds. Instead of pinning certain views on specific persons, the views can become available for all, and different people can try them on and see how they fit. If personal attachment to different possible courses of actions, or even arguments, prevents groups from examining them critically, one effective means to make these positions more neutral — the positions, not the people — is to ask other members to represent that position and develop arguments for it. This gives the group the proposal and allows the group to analyze it in terms of strengths and weaknesses. The persons attached to the position can also gain, as they find someone else developing arguments for their position.

Furthermore, by letting the group rather than one person handle the proposition, the discussion itself becomes more public, because the group will search for common values, reliable information, and shared assumptions. Public discourse means that participants have the information necessary to make a decision, that the arguments and reasons that determine the outcome are available to all, and that everyone has the opportunity to participate. For this to happen, the group needs to develop a condition of inquiry.

Condition of Inquiry

Discussions of values and assumptions can easily become so expansive and interesting that the group never makes a decision. Once people begin to examine their assumptions, they naturally also recall experiences and controversies that have shaped them. Without some guidelines, the group may begin sharing stories and philosophizing about life, which may be significant but not relevant to their task. By beginning the process of ethical reflection with the policy question, the group can accomplish its task — to arrive at a good decision about what should be done. This task, however, should not encourage participants to start judging proposals as soon as someone offers one. The final goal of the discussion is to make a judgment about what to do, but if people operate in the judgment mode all the time, then they cannot understand something new. To understand something new, we need to ask questions of inquiry rather than questions of judgment. People ask questions of judgment when they already know the answer and merely want to know if others do as well. They ask questions of inquiry when they do not know the answers and want to learn something new.

Think of someone asking you whether you would tell the truth in a particular situation. If the questioner already knows the right answer, then you feel you are the defendant and he or she is the judge. If a questioner presents a particular problem, however, and asks about the best thing to say — "How shall I tell the truth?" — then everyone can engage in a common inquiry about the conditions, values, and experiences that can serve as resources for understanding what one should do. Ethics does concern itself with making judgments — we judge what is the right thing to do — but the value of that judgment finally rests on the depth of our inquiry — on asking the right questions. If the questions of inquiry expand the discussion toward the unknown and at the same time remain connected to the policy question, then the understanding the group gains will be relevant to its task.

To decide to inquire before deciding what to do gives everyone space to ask questions and to learn more. It also overcomes defensive attitudes, especially if participants feel free to ask questions about their own proposals and even share what they see as their weaknesses as well as their strengths. Participants need to understand, in other words, that argumentative analysis is a means of investigation, not of conquering others. In summary, the group needs to know not only what is the best decision but also why. Nothing less will affirm the moral agency of the participants or develop the kind of learning environment that a responsible organization requires.

Many of these conditions cannot come into being except through the practice of ethical reflection itself. At the same time, when participants realize they are not just solving a problem or making one decision but are also establishing the necessary conditions for ethical reflection, their work will take on added significance and responsibility. Establishing these conditions, in other words, depends on the competence of all participants in the process of ethical reflection. With this in mind, let us turn to the task of training.

Training in Ethical Reflection

For ethical reflection to have relevance for organizations, it must become part of the actual decision-making process. As decision makers at different levels of the organization consider the financial, marketing, and public relations dimensions of policy proposals, they also need to consider the moral dimension. Ethical analysis, in other words, should operate as a complement to other types of analyses, so that people will have a better chance of making the right decision. The conditions for ethical reflection, therefore, are also conditions for decision making in general.

Special training in ethical reflection can ensure that decision makers at all levels have the necessary skills and conceptual tools to actively engage in the total process. Because ethics is primarily a process, we can outline a series of steps that move from formulating an issue or question to finding the answer. However we outline the map of decision making, it will not exactly match the actual process of human interaction. A map can still help us, however, especially those who have not traveled in this area before. So, a series of steps that belong to the process of ethical reflection will be presented, and you can use the worksheet and exercises in your own training.

The first step is to understand the decision-making process itself as a process of choice. What does that mean? It means that making decisions in organizations involves choosing one of several options, and doing so for some reasons. Sometimes, one proposal is the only possibility, but this rarely conforms to the actual situation. Given the particular interpretation of the situation and the particular value judgments and assumptions, one option may be necessary, but if you change these factors, you will also change the possible options. Furthermore, the meaning of moral agency, as shown in Chapter Two, assumes that persons and organizations have choices. We need to make sure that we acknowledge this aspect of the ethical perspective. The worksheet for analyzing a decision shown in Exhibit 2 has been helpful in gaining an awareness of the moral agency of decision makers.

Exhibit 2.

What decision was made? _____
_____
_____

What were the options?

1. _____
2. _____
3. _____

Why was the one option selected over the others?

1. _____
2. _____
3. _____

When participants discuss the answers they have given on the worksheet in Exhibit 2, especially in small groups, they usually discover a variety of options and selection criteria. From this experience, participants realize that when they see only one choice, they have not collected enough material to see the different options available. Furthermore, once the different choices become available, they can ask why they should choose one over another: a basic question for ethical reflection.

Once people have entered into the world of ethical reflection, so to speak, the group can then begin to develop arguments on issues that interest them. The worksheet for ethical reflections shown in Exhibit 3 can facilitate this.

Once participants have completed the worksheet in Exhibit 3, they can begin to analyze their own value judgments. In most cases, the "because" clause they wrote in their proposal statement will be some kind of descriptive statement about their observations. As we explained in Chapter Three, every sentence with a "because" clause also carries an implied premise — usually a value judgment — that connects the observation with the proposed action or policy. The group can begin its ethical analysis by discovering the implied premises in their statements. If the

Exhibit 3.

Pick three issues from your work environment that you think should be discussed or that you would like to discuss.

1. _____

2. _____

3. _____

Select one of the above three and state your proposal of what should be done. (If you do not yet have a position on the issue, select one that you think has some merit for the purpose of this exercise.)

I think we should _____

_____

because _____

_____

"because" clause is a value judgment — for example, "We should increase the quality control of our products because we must protect the safety of our customers" — then the implied observation needs to be examined. In this case, it could relate to some problems about products or their use. Once participants have begun to analyze both observations and the value judgments that connect them in developing arguments for proposed courses of action, they have already become capable of increasing the resources for making better decisions.

The next step involves handling opposing views and disagreements. The object is to find the strengths of differing views and to include them in one's own analysis of different proposals. The worksheet for developing arguments in Exhibit 4 enables participants to develop arguments against their own proposals and gives everyone a chance to argue for someone else's position. It also enables the participants to move from defending their positions to examining the merits of different positions. Participants work as partners, with each person developing his or her proposal and trading worksheets back and forth as they give reasons for and against their positions. After they have completed the dialogue, each partner writes a "because" clause at the bottom of the worksheet that takes into account the opposing views that the partners have actually developed themselves.

Exhibit 4.

Initial proposal: We should _____

_____

Partner restates your proposal: We should _____

_____

You oppose the initial proposal: We should not, because _____

_____

_____

Partner refutes your opposition: _____

_____

_____

You raise another point against your position: _____

_____

_____

Partner refutes your second objection: _____

_____

_____

You raise a third point opposing your position: _____

_____

_____

Partner refutes your third objection: _____

_____

_____

In view of the objections, write a "because" clause that supports your position. I support the initial position because _____

_____

_____

Source: Adapted from A. Stolz, 1983, p. 109.

After this exercise, participants will have the background for using the complete argumentative map shown in Exhibit 6. First, participants need to help each other answer the set of questions in the ethical reflection exercise shown in Exhibit 5, and then they can put their answers in the argumentative map shown in Exhibit 6. Again, participants should select issues that interest them from their work experiences.

Exhibit 5.

Select a controversial issue from your work. Then go through the following steps to develop the resources for developing an argument.

1. Formulate a policy or ethical question: "Should the company . . . ?"
2. Develop a policy statement: "The company should . . ."
3. State what observations or information support the policy: "Because of . . ."
4. Describe what value judgment makes the connection between the observation and information: "And because . . ."
5. Ask why you have chosen such a value judgment to connect the observation and policy. What assumptions are operative here?
6. Examine the whole argument to see if it makes sense to you.
7. Take an opposing view and develop a similar type of argument.
8. Examine the two views and pick out what you consider the strengths of each.
9. With these strengths, see if you can develop a more comprehensive and inclusive policy statement and support for it.
10. As an alternative, use the strengths to qualify your own position.
11. Use the argumentative map in Exhibit 6 to rewrite your argument.

Working with the argumentative map allows participants to develop complete arguments with explicit value judgments. Once they are familiar with this argumentative strategy, they can begin to use the traditional value judgments discussed in Chapter Five: ethics of purpose, principle, and consequence. Taking the same issues, participants can apply these and bring them into dialogue with the value judgments they have already selected. To interpret their issues or cases from the three ethical approaches, they can ask the following questions:

Exhibit 6.

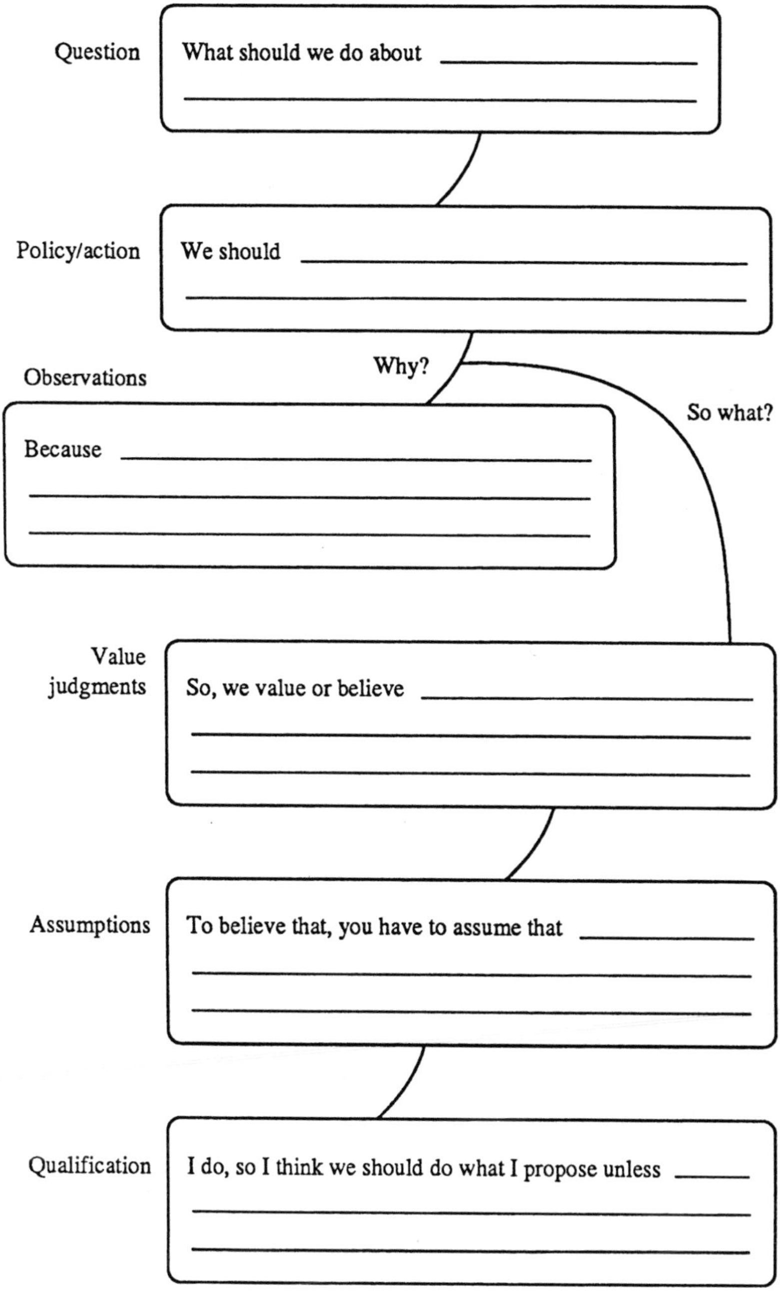

Question | What should we do about _____ _____

Policy/action | We should _____ _____

Observations

Because _____ _____ _____

Why?   So what?

Value judgments | So, we value or believe _____ _____ _____

Assumptions | To believe that, you have to assume that _____ _____ _____

Qualification | I do, so I think we should do what I propose unless _____ _____ _____

Ethics of purpose
> Who are the agents?
> What should their purposes be?
> What acts (means) will these purposes (ends) justify?

Ethics of principle
> What is the maxim (implied principle) of the action?
> Can I will that it become a universal rule that I would follow?
> Does it treat others not only as means but also as ends?

Ethics of consequence
> Who should be included in the "greatest number"?
> What are the probable consequences?
> Do the positive consequences outweigh the negative?

Once you have answered these questions, you can rewrite the arguments, using the answers to provide the policy, observations, and value judgments. They would look like Figure 20.

The final step in using these ethical traditions is to bring them together to gain a more complete understanding of the ethical dimensions of a proposed course of action. Table 2 shows what type of questions or criteria each ethical approach offers for the analysis of policy, observations, and value judgments.

Using Table 2, participants can easily see if their observations, value judgments, and proposed actions meet the criteria of all three ethical approaches. If they do not, participants may want to reframe the issue or develop new interpretations of the ethical approaches. Having participants divide into subgroups, where each group works with one ethical approach before trying to integrate all three, usually creates more resources for understanding the issues than if all the participants work together with all three. This reflective process should give participants the confidence to decide what should be done.

The next step, which will not always be required, is to see whether what should be done can be done or, in other words,

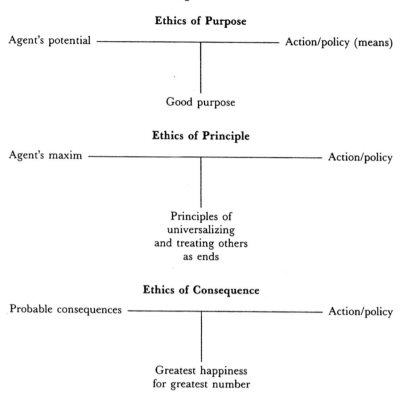

Figure 20.

Ethics of Purpose

Agent's potential ———————— Action/policy (means)

Good purpose

Ethics of Principle

Agent's maxim ———————— Action/policy

Principles of
universalizing
and treating others
as ends

Ethics of Consequence

Probable consequences ———————— Action/policy

Greatest happiness
for greatest number

Table 2.

	Observations	*Value Judgments*	*Key Assumption*
Purpose	Agent's potential or latent possibilities of being and doing	Agent's purpose	Life is purposeful, and agents can know and realize their good purpose.
Principle	Implicit maxim in proposed policy	Universalizing and reversing	Agent is willing to obey self-developed, consistent principles.
Consequence	Probable consequences	Greatest good for greatest number	Capacity to know and to measure negative and positive consequences is possible.

to examine how one's proposal aligns with the organizational systems and power relations. As was suggested in Chapter Eight, the criteria to use in evaluating the ethics of systems are justice and rights. If the system is just and individual rights are honored, then groups will have a basis for justifying their proposals. In unjust systems, in contrast, doing what is right will remain either impossible or extremely limited in scope until the system is changed.

We need to include in our training some practice in using the concepts of justice and rights in evaluating organizational systems and the distribution of power. As was demonstrated in Chapter Eight, this analysis begins with an examination of the various resources or goods distributed by the system. It then discerns how they should be distributed according to their meaning for the relevant communities — including organizational, national, and global communities. This gives us knowledge of the appropriate types of justice for different types of goods. The final step, then, is to see what individual rights belong to the different forms of justice. Or we can also reverse the order and develop an understanding of rights and then see what forms of justice they justify. In either case, the notions of justice (based on the social meaning of goods) and rights (based on the meaning of human life) can together help us understand the appropriate guidelines for designing an organizational system. To analyze your organization's practices of justice and rights, you can use the worksheet in Exhibit 7. List the goods your organization distributes in the first column, which may include everything from information to parking spaces. Then determine the types of justice that should be used in the second column, and the kind of right that corresponds to the type of justice and the distributed good in the third column. As was discussed in Chapter Eight, the five types of justice are contribution, need, membership, merit, and entitlement (see Exhibit 1). The kinds of rights are human rights, legal rights, and job-specific or contractual rights.

Agreeing on the social meaning of goods as well as the appropriate forms of justice and kind of individual rights should at least tell us what kind of system an organization should be: an organization where groups and individuals can do what is

Exhibit 7.

Goods	Types of Justice	Kinds of Rights
(Examples) Safety Wages	Equally or need Equally and contribution	Human Human and contractual

the right thing to do. This requires that the power of organizations is used justly and distributed to those who deserve it.

When participants become proficient in using the argumentative model for making decisions and in the ethical analysis of issues, they can begin to practice these competencies in the organization's decision-making processes. For this to happen, the organization itself must establish the conditions mentioned earlier, and it must also develop a culture that encourages such reflection. To make the transition from training to actual practice in ethical reflection, participants can examine their understanding of the organization's culture and its communicative patterns—subjects discussed in Chapters Nine and Ten. To use the worksheet in Exhibit 8, participants can place a mark on each line indicating their stand between the two extremes. This will allow the group to discuss their similarities and differences about each assumption. By drawing a vertical line that connects the marks on the lines, they can examine how well their assumptions fit together.

Exhibit 8.

Assumptions about:	Select a point on each continuum below and vertically connect the points to show the range of your assumptions.
Truth	Dogma • • • • • • • • • Dialogue
Promoting productivity	Theory X • • • • • • • • Theory Y
Establishing justice	Rules • • • • • • • • • Community
Meaning of work	Instrumental • • • • • • • • Intrinsic
Organizations	Instrument of domination • • • • • • • • Meaning-producing system Psychic prison • • • • • • Social contracts

For other assumptions that become important to analyze either during the process of ethical reflection or when you think of introducing ethical analysis in a decision-making process, you can develop your own worksheet. This involves the following steps:

1. State the values that connect the data and policy proposal in a particular argument.
2. Develop contrasting assumptions that seem significant for different ways to affirm the values.
3. Use the opposing alternatives as different ends of a continuum and then see where different members of the group place themselves.
4. Analyze the strengths and weakness of the assumptions by asking the following questions:
   a. Which assumptions seem most relevant to the case?
   b. Which assumptions correspond to the group's assigned task and resources?
   c. Which assumptions are most consistent with other assumptions on which the group has been working?
   d. Do some assumptions belong more to other situations than to this one?

As was explained in Chapter Ten, one of the most important assumptions concerns communication. When people imagine engaging in ethical reflection in different parts of an organization, with different groups or departments, they probably also can discern different expectations and communication habits. We can use the communications worksheet in Exhibit 9 to analyze the communication patterns in different organizational settings. It includes the dimensions of communication discussed in Chapter Nine.

Exhibit 9.

In the first column in the chart below, list eight different persons or groups with which you communicate. Include settings at work, at home, at play, and in your public and private life. Then evaluate each of the communicative relationships with the communicants on each of the following dimensions of communication, using a scale from 5 to 1 where 5 is high and 1 is low.

A. Range of topics	Many	5 4 3 2 1	Few
B. Purposes of meeting	Relational	5 4 3 2 1	Informational
C. Equality of communication	Equal	5 4 3 2 1	Unequal
D. Oral and written tradition	Oral	5 4 3 2 1	Written
E. Dimensions of meaning	Multidimensional	5 4 3 2 1	One-dimensional
F. Degree of involvement	Involved	5 4 3 2 1	Detached
G. Personal presence	Strong	5 4 3 2 1	Weak

Communicant	A	B	C	D	E	F	G

Once you have filled out the chart in Exhibit 9, you will probably find that some settings are much more conducive to ethical analysis than are others. Generally, those settings with higher numbers will be more open to ethical reflection than those with lower numbers. If some of the dimensions of communication have very high numbers—for example, a 5 on degree of involvement—they may not be conducive either, because a very strong involvement may make it more difficult for critical analysis. Group members can discuss what they see as the optimal communicative situation for raising ethical issues. Once they know the kind of situation in which they work best, they can then develop strategies to bring settings closer to their ideal. Sometimes, the awareness of different settings will enable groups to become more responsible for developing the conditions that ethical reflection needs.

If the organization develops the conditions for ethical reflection covered in the first part of this chapter, and if its members become competent in argumentative analysis and ethical reflection, then organizational ethics will become a creative and innovative human activity in the organization—one of the few activities, in fact, that maintains and even invigorates the human spirit.

Bibliography

Arendt, H. *The Human Condition*. Garden City, N.Y.: Doubleday, 1959.

Argyris, C., and Schön, D. A. *Organizational Learning: A Theory of Action Perspective*. Reading, Mass.: Addison-Wesley, 1978.

Aristotle. *Physics*. Book II.3.20–30. In R. Mckeon (ed.), *Introduction to Aristotle*. New York: Modern Library, 1947. (Originally published 335–323 B.C.)

Aristotle. *The Nicomachean Ethics*. (H. Rackham, trans.) Cambridge, Mass.: Loeb Classical Library, Harvard University Press, 1975. (Originally published 335–323 B.C.)

Arrow, K. *The Limits of Organizations*. New York: Norton, 1974.

Aune, B. *Kant's Theory of Morals*. Princeton, N.J.: Princeton University Press, 1979.

Bendix, R. *Max Weber: An Intellectual Portrait*. New York: Doubleday, 1962.

Bentham, J. *The Theory of Fictions*. In C. K. Ogden, *Bentham's Theory of Fictions*. Paterson, N.J.: Littlefield, Adams, 1959. (Originally published 1814–1827.)

Bentham, J. *An Introduction to the Principles of Morals and Legislation*. Garden City, N.Y.: Doubleday, 1961. (Originally published 1781.)

Bolman, L. G., and Deal, T. E. *Modern Approaches to Understanding and Managing Organizations*. San Francisco: Jossey-Bass, 1984.

Boulding, K. *Beyond Economics: Essays on Society, Religion, and Ethics*. Ann Arbor, Mich.: Ann Arbor Paperbacks, 1970.

Burke, K. *Language as Symbolic Action: Essays on Life, Literature, and Method*. Berkeley and Los Angeles: University of California Press, 1968.

Burke, K. *A Grammar of Motives.* Berkeley and Los Angeles: University of California Press, 1969.

Churchman, C. W. *The Systems Approach.* New York: Dell, 1968.

Churchman, C. W. *The Systems Approach and Its Enemies.* New York: Basic Books, 1979.

Clegg, S., and Dunkerley, D. *Organization, Class and Control.* London: Routledge & Kegan Paul, 1980.

Davidson, D. V., and others. *Comprehensive Business Law: Principles and Cases.* Boston: Kent, 1987.

Deal, T. E., and Kennedy, A. A. *Corporate Cultures: The Rites and Rituals of Corporate Life.* Reading, Mass.: Addison-Wesley, 1982.

Des Jardins, J. R. "Privacy in Employment." In G. Ezorsky, (ed.), *Moral Rights in the Workplace.* Albany: State University of New York Press, 1987.

Etzioni, A. *A Comparative Analysis of Complex Organizations: On Power, Involvement, and Their Correlates.* New York: Free Press, 1961.

Fisher, R., and Ury, W. *Getting to Yes: Negotiating Agreement Without Giving In.* New York: Penguin Books, 1987.

Folbre, N. *A Field Guide to the U.S. Economy: 160 Graphic Keys to How the System Works.* New York: Pantheon Books, 1987.

French, P. *Collective and Corporate Responsibility.* New York: Columbia University Press, 1984.

Fried, C. *Right and Wrong.* Cambridge, Mass.: Harvard University Press, 1978.

Galbraith, J. K. *The Anatomy of Power.* Boston: Houghton Mifflin, 1983.

Gilligan, C. *In a Different Voice: Psychological Theory and Women's Development.* Cambridge, Mass.: Harvard University Press, 1982.

Gullett, C. R., and Reisen, R. "Behavior Modification: A Contingency Approach to Employee Performance." In H. Leavitt and others (eds.). *Readings in Managerial Psychology.* (3rd ed.) Chicago: University of Chicago Press, 1980.

Gusdorf, G. *La Parole* [Speaking]. (P. T. Brockelman, trans.) Evanston, Ill.: Northwestern University Press, 1965.

Habermas, J. *The Theory of Communicative Action: Volume I: Reason and the Rationalization of Society.* (T. McCarthy, trans.) Boston: Beacon Press, 1984.

Habermas, J. *The Theory of Communicative Action: Volume II:*

Lifeworld and System: A Critique of Functionalist Reason. (T. McCarthy, trans.) Boston: Beacon Press, 1987.

Halévy, E. *The Growth of Philosophic Radicalism.* (M. Morris, trans.) Boston: Beacon Press, 1960.

Hall, B. "Collective Bargaining and Worker's Liberty." In G. Ezorsky (ed.), *Moral Rights in the Workplace.* Albany: State University of New York Press, 1987.

Harrison, R. *Bentham.* London: Routledge & Kegan Paul, 1985.

Howard, R. *Brave New Workplace.* New York: Elizabeth Sifton Books, Viking, 1985.

Kammer, C. L., III. *Ethics and Liberation: An Introduction.* Maryknoll, N.Y.: Orbis Books, 1988.

Kant, I. *The Doctrine of Virtue: Part II of the Metaphysic of Morals.* (M. J. Gregor, trans.) New York: Harper Torchbooks, 1964a. (Originally published 1797.)

Kant, I. *Groundwork of the Metaphysic of Morals.* (H. J. Paton, trans.) New York: Harper Torchbooks, 1964b. (Originally published 1785.)

Kanter, R. M. *Men and Women of the Corporation.* New York: Basic Books, 1977.

Kanter, R. M. *The Change Masters: Innovation and Entrepreneurship in the American Corporation.* New York: Simon and Schuster, 1983.

Katz, D., and Kahn, R. L. *The Social Psychology of Organizations.* (2nd ed.) New York: Wiley, 1978.

Kerr, S. "On the Folly of Rewarding A, While Hoping for B." In J. Gordon, *A Diagnostic Approach to Organizational Behavior.* Boston: Allyn and Bacon, 1983.

Laqueur, W., and Rubin, B. (eds.). *The Human Rights Reader.* New York: New American Library, 1979.

Lawrence, P. R., and Lorsch, J. W. *Organization and Environment: Managing Differentiation and Integration.* Boston: Harvard Business School Press, 1986.

Levi, M. *Thinking Economically: How Economic Principles Can Contribute to Clear Thinking.* New York: Basic Books, 1985.

Locke, J. *Second Treatise of Government.* (C. B. Macpherson, ed.) Indianapolis, Ind.: Hackett, 1980. (Originally published 1690.)

McCoy, C. S. *Management of Values: The Ethical Difference in Corporate Policy and Performance.* Boston: Pitman, 1985.

McGregor, D. *The Human Side of Enterprise.* New York: McGraw-Hill, 1960.

MacIntyre, A. *After Virtue: A Study in Moral Theory.* Notre Dame, Ind.: University of Notre Dame Press, 1981.

Macklin, R. *Mortal Choices: Ethical Dilemmas in Modern Medicine.* Boston: Houghton Mifflin, 1988.

Marx, K. *The Economic and Philosophic Manuscripts of 1844.* (D. J. Struik, ed.; M. Milligan, trans.) New York: International Publishers, 1971. (Originally published 1844.)

Maslow, A. H. "A Theory of Human Motivation." *Psychological Review,* 1943, *50,* 370–396.

Mason, R. O., and Mitroff, I. I. *Challenging Strategic Planning Assumptions.* New York: Wiley, 1981.

May, L. *The Morality of Groups: Collective Responsibility, Group-Based Harm, and Corporate Rights.* Notre Dame, Ind.: University of Notre Dame Press, 1987.

Mill, J. S. "Bentham." In M. Warnock (ed.), *John Stuart Mill: Utilitarianism, On Liberty, Essay on Bentham.* New York: World, Meridian Books, 1969. (Originally published 1838.)

Minogue, K. "The History of the Idea of Human Rights." In W. Laqueur and B. Rubin (eds.), *The Human Rights Reader.* New York: New American Library, 1979.

Moore, G. E. *Principia Ethica.* New York: Cambridge University Press, 1978. (Originally published 1903.)

Morgan, G. *Images of Organization.* Newbury Park, Calif.: Sage, 1986.

Nozick, R. *Anarchy, State, and Utopia.* New York: Basic Books, 1974.

Nye, R. D. *Three Views of Man.* Pacific Grove, Calif.: Brooks/Cole, 1975.

Ong, W. J. *Orality and Literacy: The Technologizing of the Word.* London and New York: Methuen, 1982.

O'Toole, J. *Vanguard Management: Redesigning the Corporate Future.* Garden City, N.Y.: Doubleday, 1985.

Pasmore, W. A. *Designing Effective Organizations: The Sociotechnical Systems Perspective.* New York: Wiley, 1988.

Perelman, C. *The Idea of Justice and the Problem of Argument.* (J. Petrie, trans.) New York: Humanities Press, 1971.

Perelman, C., and Olbrechts-Tyteca, L. *The New Rhetoric: A*

Treatise on Argumentation. Notre Dame, Ind.: University of Notre Dame Press, 1971.

Rand, A. *For the New Intellectual.* New York: Signet Books, 1961.

The Random House Dictionary of the English Language: The Unabridged Edition. New York: Random House, 1971.

Rawls, J. *Theory of Justice.* Cambridge, Mass.: Harvard University Press, 1971.

Robbins, S. P. *Organization Theory: Structure, Design, and Applications.* (2nd ed.) Englewood Cliffs, N.J.: Prentice-Hall, 1987.

Ross, H. *Bentham.* London: Routledge & Kegan Paul, 1983.

Schein, E. H. *Organization Culture and Leadership: A Dynamic View.* San Francisco: Jossey-Bass, 1985.

Schutz, A. *The Structures of the Life-World.* (R. M. Zaner and J. T. Engelhardt, Jr., trans.) Evanston, Ill.: Northwestern University Press, 1973.

Shklar, J. N. "Injustice, Injury, and Inequality: An Introduction." In F. S. Lucash (ed.), *Justice and Equality Here and Now.* Ithaca, N.Y., and London: Cornell University Press, 1986.

Smith, A. *An Inquiry into the Nature and Causes of the Wealth of Nations.* In R. Romano and M. Leiman, *Views on Capitalism.* (2nd ed.) Encino, Calif.: Glencoe, 1975. (Originally published 1776.)

Stolz, A. "An Exercise in Argumentation." In B. Schildgen, *Foundations in Lifelong Learning.* (2nd ed.) Minneapolis, Minn.: Burgess, 1983.

Strauss, L. *Natural Right and History.* Chicago: University of Chicago Press, 1953.

Terry, R. W. *For Whites Only.* Grand Rapids, Mich.: Eerdmans, 1970.

Toulmin, S. *The Uses of Argument.* New York: Cambridge University Press, 1957.

Toulmin, S., and others. *An Introduction to Reasoning.* (2nd ed.) New York: Macmillan, 1984.

Velasquez, M. G. "Why Corporations Are Not Morally Responsible for Anything They Do." *Business and Professional Ethics Journal,* Spring 1983, *2,* 1–17.

Velasquez, M. G. *Business Ethics: Concepts and Cases.* (2nd ed.) Englewood Cliffs, N.J.: Prentice-Hall, 1988.

Walzer, M. *Spheres of Justice: A Defense of Pluralism and Equality.* New York: Basic Books, 1983.

Index

A

Abstraction, aspects of, 104–106

Accountability: control related to, 66–68; and ethical concerns, 1; and persons as moral agents, 22

Actions: analyzing, 70–93; background on, 70–74; and behavior, ethical perspective on, 16–19; characteristic, 74, 79, 80; as a decision, 30; and ethics of consequence, 86–92; and ethics of principle, 81–86; and ethics of purpose, 74–81; focus on, 16–18; justified, 18–19; labor and work distinct from, 160; pentad for, 70–71, 93; vicarious, 29

Acton, J., 136

Affirmative action, and abstraction levels, 105–106

Agency: corporate, 28, 143–144; in decision making, 192–193. *See also* Moral agents

Agreements: and argumentative analysis, 64–69; aspects of forging, 55–69; background on, 55–57; and policy differences, 57–59; strategies for, 59–64. *See also* Disagreements

AIDS, and decision-making resources, 38–39

Alaska, and oil spill, 25

Alienation, and meaning of work, 160

Arab nations, and threats, 140

Arendt, H., 160

Argumentative analysis: and agreements, 64–69; and decision making, 6–7, 41, 47–49; and ethical reflection, 6–7, 48, 54; and ethics of consequence, 92; and ethics of princi-

ple, 85–86, 92; and ethics of purpose, 77, 92; example of, 50–53; map for, 196–198; for qualification of opposing views, 63

Arguments: developing, 194–195; *ethos, logos,* or *pathos* for, 185–187

Argyris, C., 3

Aristotle, 74–76

Arrow, K., 141

Assumptions: and actions, 77, 85, 91; analyzing, 10–12; analyzing differences between values and, 147–167; another's, 152; attributes of, 36–37; awareness of, 150–153; background on, 147–150; basic, 21–29; concept of, 10, 147–148; about consequences, 166–167; and culture, 148, 150; as decision-making resource, 31–32, 33; different, and shared values, 153–164; of ethics, 16; evaluation of, 155–156; on excellence, 158–160; and expressive terms, 40, 42; investigating differences in, 151–152; on justice, 157–158; on nature of organizations, 161–163; and options development, 153; on productivity, 156–157; and reality, 21–29; on self-esteem, 165–166; shared, and different values, 164–167; taking a stand on, 57; on truth finding, 153–155; value judgments distinct from, 20–22; voices from subcultures for, 152; worksheet for, 201–202

Authority, topology of, and truth, 154

B

Bad-apple fallacy, 1